Tears for Tyler

MONIQUE PATTERSON

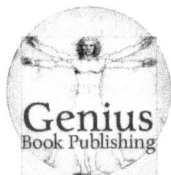

Genius
Book Publishing

Los Angeles, California, USA

Published by:
Genius Book Publishing
31858 Castaic Road #154
Castaic, CA 91384
GeniusBookPublishing.com

Photos of Tyler Dean courtesy of Jeynelle Dean-Hayes.
Photos of Judeland Anthony courtesy of Judeland Anthony.
Photos of Alicia Little courtesy of Lee Little.
All photos used with permission.

Don't Cry Mum by John F. Connor used with permission.

For more information on this case or to reach out to the author, please email
moniquerpatterson@gmail.com

ISBN: 978-1-947521-38-4

200903

Don't cry mum
By John F. Connor

Don't cry mum please don't be sad
Think back to the fun we had
Don't cry mum please don't be blue
You cannot see me but I see you

I walk beside you everyday
I never really went away
I am with you morning noon and night
When you are sad I hold you tight

Don't cry mum I am ok
And we will meet again some day
One day when the time is right
I will be waiting in the light

But you have a life to live
So much love you have to give
Don't cry mum I love you so
More than you will ever know

Speak to me and I will hear
Never far I am always near
The bond we share was oh so strong
I am still here I have not gone

Preface

On a cool autumn day in Warrnambool in south-west Victoria, I get a text message on my phone. *We're at the service station, we'll be there in five minutes,* it reads. I'm nervous. Not the type of "I don't want to do this nervous," more the "I'm about to go to a job interview for a role I really want and I don't want to mess it up nervous." A car pulls into my driveway and I check for the 90th time that I have my notebook, a pen (the amount of times I've gone to interview someone without a pen is something that shall remain a secret, but I'll admit it's more than once) and check that my iPhone is fully charged. I jump in the car and instantly recognise Jeynelle Dean-Hayes. We've never met in person, only spoken on the phone, but I recognise her from photos in newspaper articles and television interviews. She introduces me to her husband Josh. I comment that's it's chilly. If I had to guess I'd say maybe 16 or 17 degrees, but I've never really been one for checking a weather forecast. All I can say is that it is a cold Warrnambool morning. The coastal city is dubbed windy Warrnambool and that always adds to the chill factor. They have driven nearly two hours to talk to me and while we would usually arrange to chat at a café or a restaurant over coffee, coronavirus dictates that we have to be creative. Cafes are open for takeaways only. In our Facebook messages in the days leading up to our meeting, I have suggested Thunder Point. This is a popular tourist attraction in the city—a car park where you can watch the waves crash against the rocks below. You can also look out over the city's breakwater and secluded Lady Bay. We make small talk on the short drive. I find out that Josh is an actor. An out-of-work actor due to COVID-19. We arrive at Thunder Point and they sort of turn around in their seats. Jeynelle, obviously the most sensible of the three of us, decides that perhaps we should go for a walk. When we get out of the car she heads to the boot of the car. She points to a decal on the back window. *Tyler Dean, 1999-2017 RIP. Fly high beautiful Angel*, it reads. She later tells me that the same decal adorns dozens of cars in Geelong and Melbourne. Jeynelle gingerly grabs an oversized grey pencil case from the boot. We head towards the lookout and briefly look out at the sea. We begin to talk about her beautiful boy. We're looking out at the ocean but if you ask me whether it was rough or flat that day I wouldn't be able to answer, not even under oath. Josh looks around for seats but there are none. Jeynelle suggests we "camp down here."

So we do. Jeynelle and I sit cross-legged and talk for more than two hours straight. Josh occasionally adds a detail, a funny story about the young man whose life was tragically cut short. The odd tourist heads to the lookout, probably looking at us wondering what has us so enthralled. We don't look up, not even to make niceties like I know both of us usually would. Even if one of the tourists had yelled that they spotted a southern right whale breaching below, as they are known to do in waters off Warrnambool, I don't think either of us would have averted our eyes to the water—not even for a moment.

I already know some of the story that Jeynelle is telling me. I know that Tyler was the victim of a hit and run accident and that Jeynelle and Josh are appalled with the way it was handled. I also know that they were so incensed by one aspect of the law in Victoria that they fought to have it changed—and won. Jeynelle reveals that the grey pencil case is jam-packed full of photos of a smiling Tyler. His cheeky blue eyes shine out at me. She tells me about the mischief he would find himself in. She longingly looks at a handwritten note from Tyler that simply tells her he loves her. I suggest I could take some photos of the items with my iPhone but she hands over the pencil case to me. I vow inwardly to guard this bag of treasures with my life. It sits in my cupboard now. I know that if god forbid my house caught fire it would be the one item I grab after my two sons.

When our conversation begins to come to a close, I comment that the sun has been shining on us the whole time. This is rare for a Warrnambool morning at this time of year. *Perhaps it's Tyler keeping us warm,* I comment. *Yes,* Jeynelle replies with a broad smile. We hug, despite the fact this is a big no-no in these current pandemic times, both willing to suffer the consequences if there are any. She has just bared her soul to me and I have vowed to share her son's story. I know that it is a story that needs to be told. What I don't know yet is that I am about to discover that Australia has a justice system that is failing so many hit and run victims. What I don't know yet is that Jeynelle was right to push for a law change. Because, as she tells me often, car crime is treated as a joke—and not just in Australia.

Chapter 1

Larger than life is a term that is more often than not an exaggeration. It's a way of conveying an electric spark that someone possesses in one way or another. But one person who truly embodied the term was Tyler Dean. What he lacked in stature he made up for in every other aspect of his life. "He was always on the go," laughs his mother Jeynelle Dean-Hayes. From a very young age it became clear that Tyler

thought sleep was a waste of time. Life was for
the living and he did everything he could to fit
in as much as he could to each and every day.
Tyler was the younger brother of Samuel, who
was eight when Tyler was born. Jeynelle said
she knew straight away that the two siblings
were chalk and cheese. "Samuel is such a calm
person," she said. Tyler, on the other hand,
had a mischievous smile and a knack for
getting himself into trouble. When Tyler was
a teenager, it was not uncommon for Jeynelle
to find a card in the mailbox asking her to
bring her son down to the local police station.
Luckily, the family had moved from Geelong
to the smaller town of Winchelsea and there
wasn't too much strife he could get into. More
often than not he had been called into the
police station because he and his mates had
decided to spray paint something on a whim
or had damaged property while engaging in
the typical larrikin behaviour that teenage
boys in groups often do. "Once," Jeynelle
says with a smile on her face, "Tyler found
himself in trouble for doing something he

thought was the right thing to do at the time. There was a cat that was being kept in a cage down the street," Jeynelle said. "He felt sorry for it and let it out." That was Tyler's nature. Loving, kind, gentle and always testing the limits. So loving that he didn't mind telling his mum how much he loved her and was always reaching out for a hug, no matter who was around. One day he took exception with a mate who sniggered when he told his mum he loved her and gave her a hug. "There was one kid who hadn't been to our place before," Jeynelle said. Tyler walked in and as he always did he hugged his mum and told her he loved her. When he heard his mate laugh at his expense, he made it clear he wasn't going to take that sort of attitude. "Tyler, who was a little pocket rocket because he hadn't shot up, turned around and stomped across the floor to this kid who was three feet taller and asked him what he was laughing at." The stunned mate told him it was because he had hugged his mum and told him he loved her. "He said 'Yeah I hug my mum, I love my mum, what are you going to do about it?' That was Tyler," says Jeynelle. "A free spirit who loved his family and would fight to the death for them. Every day for the rest of his life if he needed to."

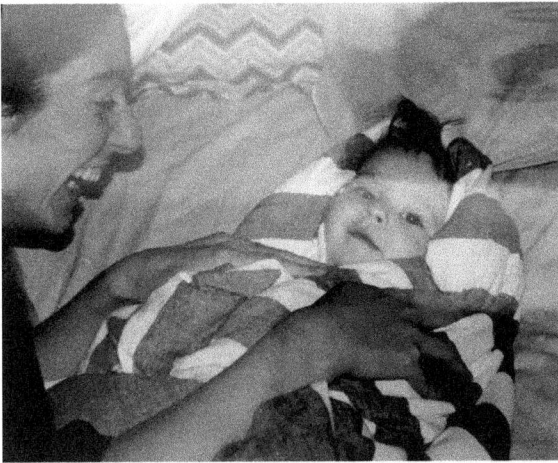

Chapter 2

Tyler Simon Dean was born at 5.31am at the William Angliss Hospital in Melbourne on January 2, 1999. He was the second son for Jeynelle Hayes and the first for Simon Lamb. He weighed seven pounds, three ounces and had the most beautiful blue eyes his parents had ever seen. Tyler's older brother Samuel had weighed over nine pounds and Jeynelle was shocked at how tiny her new bundle of joy was. "I was afraid I was going to break him, he was that little," she said. Like many battles that she would wage on Tyler's behalf in later life, she had to beg a particularly nasty nurse to call her doctor and tell him she was in labour. "I went into labour on New Year's Day," she said. "I woke up about 6am and I thought 'that doesn't feel right.' I wasn't in pain, it was just sort of this twinge.'" Jeynelle said she went about her daily household routine until about 4pm when she was convinced she was in labour. Having been brought up on a farm, and having a 'just get on with things' attitude, she continued with her plans for the night. "At about 9.30pm I was cooking a shepherd's pie in the kitchen between contractions," she said. "I didn't have an egg so I walked down to my friend's house on the corner to get an egg, breathing through the contractions." When the pain became worse about 11pm she ran herself a bath. "We rang the hospital and they said 'No, probably don't come in yet.'" By 1am Jeynelle knew she had to get to the hospital—and fast. "I thought 'I'm going to give birth in the car because we had to drive from Wantirna South to Ferntree Gully." The couple arrived at the hospital, keen to welcome their new baby. But a nurse on a power trip had other plans. "She looked me over and said 'You're not in labour.'" She then proceeded to tell the then 22-year-old that when she was older she would be better equipped to recognise the signs. Jeynelle, having given birth to Samuel eight years before, was incensed by this. "I said 'I have been through this before.'" But the nurse was having none of it. She told a horrified Jeynelle and Simon to go home and come back later. Jeynelle refused. "I'm not going," she told the nurse matter-of-factly. "It got to about 3.30am and I went back to the nurse because I was in agony. I said 'You either fix this or I'll take care of it myself.'" Jeynelle's icy stare must have been enough to prompt the nurse into action because she called the doctor. He confirmed that Jeynelle was in labour and that Tyler was in fact in distress. "They broke my water for me and he was out. Done. Straight away. I was furious." She couldn't believe that a nurse—a person tasked with helping others—had put the life of her unborn child at risk because she assumed Jeynelle was young and stupid.

Chapter 3

Tyler knew how to suck the marrow out of life and he did this in the short time he was on earth. Anyone who knows someone like this can tell you that their very presence makes you smile. Jeynelle and her husband Josh—Tyler's stepfather—are grateful for every second they had with the loveable maverick. "We realise how blessed we were to have him for the time we did," Jeynelle says. She laments that she will never have the chance to watch her youngest son become a husband or father. But she knows that Tyler had defied the odds once before. When he was about six months old, Jeynelle put him and Samuel in the car and headed out in the busy streets of Bayswater in Melbourne to pick up a highchair. On the way back an 81-year-old driver pulled out in front of Jeynelle. "He was in the u-turn bay in the middle and he didn't see us coming down the hill," she said. "He just pulled out and I had nowhere to go. I slammed straight into the back of him." Dazed and terrified, Jeynelle called out to Samuel to see if he was okay and turned around to see a horrific sight in the backseat. "The impact was so hard that Tyler's car seat was upside down," she recalled in horror. Fearing the worst, she jumped out of the car to right the upturned car seat. "He wasn't screaming. That was the most terrifying thing," she said. "The car was full of white dust from the airbag and I was screaming at Samuel to get out of the car because I thought it was going to explode. I flipped over Tyler's car seat and he was white. He wasn't blinking, he wasn't crying. I thought 'my baby is gone' and I just flipped out." Then, in what Jeynelle would recall as the most beautiful sound for decades to come, the tiny infant took a deep breath. He was alive. After embracing her youngster, Jeynelle's mother instincts kicked in and she wanted to give the elderly driver a piece of her mind. But onlookers held her back. The two boys recovered well. Jeynelle, on the other hand, developed agoraphobia. She was also diagnosed with PTSD and severe depression. "I wasn't able to leave the house," Jeynelle said. "I would step onto the front porch and get so dizzy I would almost pass out," she said. "Some days I couldn't raise my head off the pillow." Jeynelle had the two most important people by her side—her sons—and she didn't want to risk their lives again. However, her haven from the world soon became more like a war zone. Her partner became addicted to pain medication after injuring his back at work. "Soon, taking it orally wasn't enough and he began injecting it," she said. "I left permanently when I found syringes hidden in Tyler's toy box," she said. Despite Jeynelle's fears of the outside world, she knew her boys deserved better. "He was treating me terribly and I couldn't take it anymore," she said. "I thought, 'If I can't get out of this house how am I supposed to get the kids away from him?'" Jeynelle summoned all of her strength and decided to leave. Her resolve would see her bond with her boys grow even stronger.

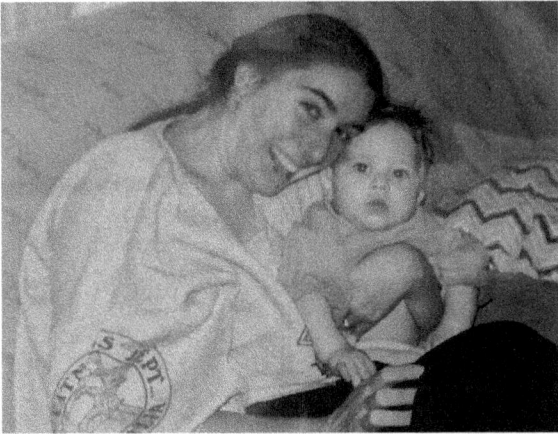

Chapter 4

Early on it was clear Tyler had a stubborn streak, much like his mother. "He was such a finicky baby," Jeynelle says. He was like a tornado; always on the go. Even as a toddler. "He didn't rest. Ever," Jeynelle says. His grandmother Ellen Dean would rock him and sing Heidi-Ho (the elephant song) to him in a bid to put him to sleep. Convinced she had won the battle with the infant determined to stay awake, she would carefully carry him to his room and place him in his bassinet. "She would go to walk out and put her hand on the doorknob, turn around and he would be laying there staring at her as if to say 'Where are you going?'" He would gaze at her with his big blue eyes and she knew that it was another lost battle. Ellen recalls singing that song to Tyler hundreds of times when he was an infant. But she couldn't stay frustrated with Tyler for long. No one could.

School wasn't a good fit for Tyler. He loved the interaction with mates but would much rather be busy using his hands. He loved cars and taking things apart. In fact, to this day, Jeynelle and Josh still stumble across the odd bolt or spark plug on the lawn—a piece that went astray during one of Tyler's many DIY projects. "He loved cars," Josh says. "He loved to dismantle things." He was oblivious to it but he was [also] quite a hit with the ladies. On one visit to a shopping centre, Jeynelle remembers a group of girls who became excited at the sight of her son. "They said, 'Look! It's

Tyler.'" Cool as a cucumber he walked over to the group, who proceeded to shower him with praise and affection. When the pair left, Jeynelle was laughing at the encounter. Tyler told her, somewhat embarrassed, "They all keep telling me I'm so cute and adorable. But it's only because I'm short." Jeynelle told him he would look back at the moment and miss the attention. Tyler shrugged.

When the family moved to Winchelsea, a small town about 40 kilometres outside of Geelong, Tyler was disappointed. He was worried he would miss his mates. But Jeynelle and Josh hoped the smaller town would give Tyler less opportunities to get himself in trouble. He quickly made friends and their zest for life and impulsive behaviour did result in them catching the eye of local police on more than one occasion. But his transgressions—perhaps riding without a helmet—usually only earnt him a slap on the wrist.

As a young boy Tyler had more to deal with than most children his age. His interaction with his father—who battled with drug addiction for years—was limited. Then, in 2010, tragedy struck. Simon Lamb was found unconscious in the gutter outside the front of his house. He died in the ambulance but was revived by paramedics. Unfortunately, he was declared brain dead at the hospital and his life support was switched off. He had overdosed on drugs. "I remember hugging him goodbye after and I put my hand on the large tattoo of Tyler's name over his heart," Jeynelle said. "It was devastating." Tyler was grief-stricken and angry. "He went through a bit of a struggle," Jeynelle said. "He asked 'Why wouldn't my dad give up drugs for me?'"

When Simon died Jeynelle thought she may have had a sort of premonition about it. Months before she had woken crying. She had just had the worst nightmare possible. In it she couldn't find Tyler. She was walking aimlessly through a field when she came across his lifeless body. Next to him was a bike. When Jeynelle woke up she immediately burst into tears. And she cried for days. She cried at work. She cried at lunch. She cried more than she had ever cried before. Then when she learnt the horrible news that the father of her youngest son had died, she thought that perhaps the dream had been about him. Now, every day when she opens her eyes, she wishes that the events of October 18, 2017 were just that. A nightmare. But sadly her eerie prediction came true.

Tyler never had trouble making friends. One of his school mates, Darcy Young, considered him more than a best mate. He considered him a brother for life. The two would talk for hours and Darcy remembers that his mate's smile would light up any room. He also remembers that Tyler wasn't afraid to speak his mind. Darcy's girlfriend Lola Eishold said Darcy was devastated to lose his mate. Tyler "was a good kid," she said. "He would help anyone out, even if they were a stranger." She said she had no doubt Tyler would have been well-known in years to come. "He enjoyed life and it's sad he wasn't able to accomplish his dreams," Lola said.

Sam Bushby met Tyler when he was 13 or 14. His dad lived in Winchelsea and Sam spent weekends in the town. One day he went to the pool and saw a young Tyler—who would have been 9 or 10—being bullied by a number of other kids. "I said something to the kids to get them to leave him alone," Sam said. He then introduced himself to Tyler. Despite the age gap, they became best mates. "We were mates after that day," Sam said. "Every weekend I was at dad's hanging out with Tyler."

Sam said his friend was "amazing." In fact, he said he owes his life to his younger friend. Sam has suffered depression and said his mate was always there for him. "I had my heart broken and thought about taking my life," Sam said. "Tyler sang *Superman* by Eminem," Sam remembers, trying to remind him that there were more fish in the sea. Sam couldn't help but laugh. Tyler and Sam would watch YouTube videos, play video games, and walk and talk for hours. Sam said his nan dubbed him "the wanderer" because he and Tyler would walk around Geelong for hours on end. They just walked around, talking, with no real plans, for five to six hours. These were some of the best days of Sam's life. They also got into their fair share of trouble. Sam remembers they decided to camp in Tyler's backyard. They set up a tent and using an extension cord they hooked up the game console so they could do what they usually did in Tyler's bedroom. That night Tyler told Sam about a neighbour who had a fridge in his backyard stocked with alcohol. Sam said Tyler was nervous about swiping some stubbies and drinking them. So Sam did the dirty work. "I crept over there, grabbed as many drinks as I could, and we drank them," Sam said. He said his younger mate became even more animated than usual after a few beers and vodka cruisers.

"I got into a lot of trouble because of him, but I don't blame him," Sam remembers with a smile. Sam said he often went to bat for his younger mate. "I would do anything for Tyler," he said. Sam said he considered Tyler a brother for life and Jeynelle a second mother. He also credits Tyler for introducing him to his favourite show *Adventure Time*. Not that he watches it too often these days. The memories it sparks are too much to bear. "We used to watch it together for hours," he said. Sam remembers the two promised each other they would be in each other's lives forever. "I said, 'You're not allowed to die before me.' We promised each other."

When Josh entered their mother's life, Tyler had initial reservations. He questioned whether he had to answer to his stepfather. But this wasn't a surprise, given the fact he had only ever known his mum to be on her own. When it became clear that Josh made his mum happy and loved her sons as his own, Tyler and Samuel embraced him as their stepfather. When the two married, Tyler was elated. Both boys were ring bearers on the big day. "Tyler gave me Josh's ring and Samuel gave Josh mine," Jeynelle said. "It was their part of 'giving me away' after Dad walked me down the aisle." Tyler had a great time and shared his happiness on social media. "Congratulations mum and Josh hope yous are happy forever," he wrote on his Facebook page on their wedding day."

In the last months of his life, Tyler had much to celebrate. He had just signed a contract to begin an apprenticeship as a panel beater. In addition to that, he had been gifted the thing that teenage males dream of, his own car. On his 18th birthday, his mother was beyond excited to show him his present—a second-hand car. Rubbing his eyes, he at first thought it was a joke. "You're fucking with me!" he exclaims on a home video of the moment. "It's yours, I just bought it," Jeynelle replied. "Is this a prank?" Tyler asks. "It's wicked. Fuckin' mad. It's cool." On that day much gratitude and hugs followed.

Tyler was a teenager who rebelled against typical norms. He loved to dye his hair in shades of black or purple, wore spacer earrings, had a lip ring, and smoked marijuana. His mum and stepfather have never shied away from these facts. They knew he smoked marijuana. They didn't condone it, but they had a decision to make. "Put our foot down and potentially drive him to smoke in risky situations or allow him to smoke in his caravan outside where he was safe," Jeynelle said. "We chose his safety." Jeynelle was pleased that Tyler had decided to try to give up marijuana because he feared a random drug test at his apprenticeship and he didn't want anything to get in the way of realising his dream.

Tyler had a few girlfriends over the years and had most recently been seeing a girl named Steph. Jeynelle remembers cleaning up her son's room because he told her she was going to come over. He was impressed with her efforts. When Tyler died, Stephanie and her mum sent Jeynelle an angel bear, which she carried in the Shine a Light on Road Safety march. She now takes that bear to every family occasion and it sits in Tyler's chair. "He's a very special bear and Stephanie is a very special girl," she said.

Jeynelle remembers countless nights when she would tell Tyler to go to sleep. She works night shifts at home and would always hear Tyler listening to music and talking to his friends on Skype. At the time she would wish he would turn his music down and go to sleep.

Now she would give anything to hear his sweet voice chatting to his mates or hear the familiar creak of the pantry opening. That was a noise she would hear countless times a day. Tyler, always on the go, loved snacks. In fact, that was a topic that came up in mother and son's final conversation.

A look at Tyler's Facebook page paints the picture of a young man who loves cars, motorbikes, is constantly looking for someone to catch up with or chat to and who has a wicked sense of humour. You can't help but chuckle at the memes and sayings he shared such as "After I give advice, I always end my sentence with 'idk tho' so you can never say I ruined your life." In a video he shared, an adult is trying to decipher teen speak by asking who is "lmfao." Another post is a Facebook message supposedly from the Ontario Rainbow Alliance of the Deaf. "Hi Kevin, I'm seeing a voice message, what's going on?" the post reads. "This is a deaf organisation. Could you please write down what it says." Another one, which is this author's favourite, is of a court scene. A lawyer is questioning a police officer. "A woman shot her husband because he stepped on her freshly mopped floor," the lawyer states to the police officer. "That's correct," the officer replies. "And it took you 20 minutes to arrest her. Why?" he asks. "The floor was still wet."

Tyler also shares photos of family and friends and posts numerous times asking what people are up to or asking them to like his post. On September 20, 2017, Tyler posted a selfie. In it he was wearing a shirt and trousers. "Good day handing in resumes," he posted with a grin on his face.

Chapter 5

On the third Wednesday of October in 2017, Tyler had a spring in his step. He was set to hand in the contract for his apprenticeship at South City Panels in Geelong during his lunch break. He would soon be taking the first steps towards realising his dream of becoming a panel beater. Jeynelle and Josh had a busy day too. Josh, an actor, was filming footage for a competition at a number of different locations.

One place he wanted to film at was the North Geelong Train Station. They needed an extra pair of hands and Jeynelle suggested they ask Tyler. He could meet them at the station and get a lift home with them rather than catching the train back to Winchelsea. However, Tyler wasn't too keen on the idea. "He sent a message back and said, 'I'm really knackered, it's been a big day.'" Tyler told his mum he just wanted to go home and "veg out." Initially Jeynelle wasn't too pleased. "I cracked it a little bit and said, 'We really need your help with this.' But when he again said he was too tired, she relented, telling Tyler they would get someone else to help out. "We told him, it's okay, we've found someone else. We hadn't but we didn't want him to feel bad." Tyler replied to the text, relieved his mum wasn't angry. He told her to let them know if they still needed help later on and he would try to come back into Geelong. Later, when the couple was at the station, Tyler called his mum for a chat. "He called about 7.20pm and we actually had an amazing chat," Jeynelle said. "It was such a good talk. I told him we had been shopping and I had bought him a heap of snacks." Tyler told his mum she was a legend and told her he loved her. "I told him, 'When we get home Josh wants to make homemade burgers and he said 'That's awesome.'" Jeynelle then hung up the phone and the two began the drive home. They stopped at a rest stop to film some more footage and arrived home in Winchelsea about 9.40pm. Tyler wasn't home.

"We pretty much both cracked a beer and sat down on the bed and then saw lights through the window," Josh said. He looked out the window and saw a police car. "We didn't think anything of it," Jeynelle said. "We thought 'Tyler's got himself in bloody trouble again, probably riding without a helmet or something.'" Jeynelle went to the front door and was asked if she was Tyler Dean's mum. "I said, 'Yeah what's the little bugger done now?' That's the first thing I said." The officers asked Jeynelle if she was home alone. "That was the first minute I got a twinge," Jeynelle said. "I said, 'No, my hubby's in the bedroom,' and they asked me to go and get him. That's when I really started to think. I was thinking, 'We're going to be spending a lot of time at the hospital.'" Jeynelle went and opened the bedroom door. She told Josh the police wanted to speak to him as well. She remembers the moment vividly. "He didn't say a word. I'll never forget that for as long as I live. I looked at Josh, Josh looked at me. Not a word was spoken." They returned to the lounge room together. Jeynelle remembers sitting on the arm of the couch while Josh stood. The police officers told them they were from Colac. "They said we need to let you know there was a crash tonight and Tyler was involved and he didn't make it." Dumbfounded, Jeynelle replied, "What?! I don't understand." Again, one of the officers repeated that there had been a crash and Tyler didn't make it. "They never said he was dead, they just said he didn't make it," Jeynelle remembers. At that moment the room began spinning and voices came in and out, Josh said. "You know those scenes in a movie where a bomb goes off and everyone's ears are ringing and everything is in slow motion? It was sort of like that," he said. Jeynelle, however, didn't believe what she was hearing. "I said, 'No, your information is wrong. Tyler is at a friend's place. It must be someone else that you've got out there.'" The officers told Jeynelle her son had been identified by his friend Oaklee Leamer at the scene. The shellshocked couple was told by the officers they would stay at their home while they notified family about the tragedy. Jeynelle, still struggling to believe her youngest son would never come home, said she didn't want to go to the crash scene. "You hear of people who want to race out to the scene but I never wanted to," she said. "Not for a second did I want to go out there. If he was gone then going out there wasn't going to help in any way and I knew I would see something I didn't want to see. That's not how I wanted to remember him." Jeynelle will be grateful to those officers, but she is perplexed that the couple has never heard from any of their local police officers in their small town.

"Perhaps it's because of their previous dealings with Tyler," Jeynelle suggests. But it still hurts. "They didn't do the notification, they didn't come to check on us, they didn't come to tell us someone had been arrested."

In the minutes and hours that followed, Jeynelle and Josh tried desperately to reach their parents and Samuel. It seemed that no one was in a hurry to answer their phone that night. Terrified that Samuel would hear the news from someone else, or see it on social media, Jeynelle continued to call her oldest son. "It was hard because they all answered the phone the same way. They said 'Hey, how are you?' and they were so pleased to hear from us.'" Sadly, the words that would follow the initial greeting would shatter their happy lives forever. Samuel, like his mother, initially didn't believe the news. "When I told him Tyler didn't make it, he said 'What? What do you mean?' His brain wouldn't take it in." Sadly, the family's horrific ordeal was just beginning.

I love you all 🤍🤍🤍

Chapter 6

Rather than stay in Geelong, Tyler had headed home that night to relax. But in true Tyler fashion, he couldn't sit still for long. When his mate Oaklee messaged Tyler to see if he wanted to go with him to look at a motorbike, he quickly agreed. Oaklee decided to buy the pit bike and they then decided to go to another mate's house. At some point that night they smoked a small amount of marijuana but

Tyler hadn't been drinking. The two returned to Tyler's house so that he could pick up his own motorised bike. The plan was for them to meet up once Tyler grabbed his bike then head on to Glenn "Spitty" Lewis' house. He lived a few kilometres out of town, but it was a trip they had done on numerous occasions. At about 8.15pm they met up again and headed out of town. "It was fairly dark," Oaklee said. "It wasn't pitch black but it was fairly dark." Neither Tyler nor Oaklee had lights on their bikes but the flat road made it easy to see oncoming vehicles. The sound of the engines on their bikes meant chatter wasn't possible between them. Oaklee went ahead of Tyler and got the scare of his life when a four-wheel-drive narrowly missed hitting him. The vehicle was driving in the middle of the road and its lights were off, Oaklee said. "It—he nearly hit me. I didn't really see it until it was right beside me." Oaklee, shaken by the driver's actions, stopped to wait for his mate to catch up. "I stopped in the middle of the road," he said. "I waited for Tyler but he never came." Oaklee was puzzled. He knew his friend wasn't far behind him. He turned around and rode back the way he had come in search of Tyler. The scene that he came across would haunt him for the rest of his life.

"I was following the white line, um, until I got to Tyler's body, um, which I had to swerve not to hit, mind you." Panic-stricken, he grabbed his mobile phone for light and ran to his mate's side. In that moment he noticed a car some distance down the road. The action of the driver turning the lights on and then off had caught his attention. Then the car drove off. Oaklee tried in vain to get a response from Tyler. "I was crying, I was screaming, I was yelling out to him," Oaklee said. "He didn't respond at all." With shaking hands, Oaklee called Glenn. "I dunno how far from Spitty's we were, but I knew we were really close because we had been on the road for a little bit. Um, so I called Spitty straight away, told him to come down." Oaklee struggled to explain to him what had happened. "I was crying. He couldn't really understand me."

Glenn, who is in a wheelchair after a motorbike accident in 1994, was watching television in his unit when Oaklee called him. "He said Tyler's been hit, he's been hit, come quick," Glenn said. "He was bawling... and he was very hysterical." Oaklee didn't say where they were, but Glenn jumped in his car and went in search of them. "He didn't say where he was but I had an idea he must be on the road from his mum's house to mine," Glenn said.

Meanwhile, back at the incident, a police car had arrived. The officers from Anglesea were on their way to another job and just happened to come across the accident site. Sergeant Craig Stanton was on patrol with Leading Senior Constable Trevor Purcell that night. When they turned left into Aitkins Road, Sergeant Stanton remarked to his colleague that there was what appeared to be a haze on the road in front of them. The two then saw a light shining towards them. "I mentioned to Purcell that it looked like there might have been a bit of smoke over the

roadway," Sergeant Stanton said. "But as we
got closer the torch light was flashing towards
us." Sergeant Purcell thought at first there may
be a cow on the road and someone was trying
to warn them. As the two officers got closer
to the accident scene, a hysterical Oaklee ran
up to the police car. "I opened the door and
he was yelling that his friend had been run
over," Sergeant Stanton said. "He was totally
distraught," Sergeant Purcell added. The
officers radioed in to D24 for back-up and
went to check on Tyler.

"At that point I didn't know what his
condition was, but on actually sighting [the
victim], who I now know to be Tyler Dean,
it was evident from his injuries that he was
deceased." The officers quickly closed to the
road to traffic and established a crime scene.
Oaklee told the officers his friend had been hit
by a large dark vehicle with a bull bar. He told
them the vehicle's lights were not on and that
the driver of the car had not stopped. Sergeant
Stanton said he didn't observe any skid marks
at the scene. He saw debris on the side of the

road—scattered pieces of Tyler's bike—and noticed Tyler wasn't wearing shoes and his helmet was resting in the grass.

Oaklee then called his own mother. "I said that Tyler had been hit by a car and that he was dead," Oaklee said. His mother Melanie Leamer recalled receiving the call from her devastated son about 10 minutes after he had left on his motorbike. She grabbed her keys but her partner Christian knew she was in no state to drive. "My whole body was shaking," Melanie said.

By the time Glenn arrived at the accident scene, there were a number of police cars. Oaklee quickly came to Glenn's car and jumped in. He hugged his older mate. "He was breaking down real bad and he was a complete mess," Glenn said. When Melanie and her partner arrived at the accident scene, Oaklee rushed to embrace them. "He was saying that Tyler was dead," Melanie said. "He just kept repeating it. And we asked what happened and he said that there was a car driving down the road with no headlights on and it hit him."

When Sergeant Stanton was handed a mobile phone by a woman at the crash scene, he was puzzled. The woman, Kerrianne Hogan, told the officer that Billy-Jay Glynn was on the phone. Sergeant Stanton asked, "Who is it?" Kerrianne told him that it was her son. Confused, the officer pointed to Tyler, thinking she meant he was her son. Instead, she told him, "No, my son did that." Sergeant Stanton took the phone but couldn't understand what the man on the other end was trying to tell him. He told Glynn to stay put, that a police car would go to his residence. Sergeant Stanton asked Hogan how she knew to come to the scene. "He told me," she said, referring to her son. That night Glynn was arrested for the hit and run death of Tyler Dean.

"And I'd choose you;
in a hundred lifetimes,
in a hundred worlds,
in any version of reality,
I'd find you and I'd choose you.
-The Chaos of Stars

Always Loved
Never Forgotten

02.1.99-18.10.17

Chapter 7

The days that followed Tyler's death were a living nightmare for his family and friends. Jeynelle is forever grateful that Josh took care of most of the plans for Tyler's funeral. He pored over photos and videos of the vivacious teenager and put together a memorial video that would leave everyone at the service in tears. Josh wrote on his Facebook page that he couldn't believe Tyler was gone. "This is difficult to type out as my hands are still shaking from the visit from two very compassionate, very professional members of the Colac police," he wrote. "Last night, our son Tyler was taken away from us—the only reason I'm able to type this is because it doesn't yet seem real, nothing does. I'm waiting… hoping to be the butt of some practical joke or there has been some kind of clerical error. However, a clerical error would mean someone else would go on to receive this gutting, soul-crushing news, which I have no wish for anyone ever to receive." Josh said he didn't believe there was a word that could describe the rage, despair, and numbness running through him. "Tyler just finished putting the signature on his paperwork the day before; he was accepted into a four-year apprenticeship and he was nothing short of 'pumped' to get started." Josh urged parents to hug their children. "You never know when there will be a last hug," he wrote. "For now Tyler, I'll see you later."

Jeynelle wondered how she could go on. "My darling Tyler, I haven't slept," she wrote on Facebook on October 19. "I don't know how I'm supposed to open my eyes each day and know you aren't here to hug me and tell me you love me each time you race out the door or hang up the phone. I have loved you madly every day of your life. I will never stop even though you are waiting in Heaven for me now. Sleep well baby."

Hundreds of people attended Tyler's funeral on October 30. The song *Heaven is a Halfpipe* was one of the songs played to celebrate his life. Jeynelle, while furiously wiping away tears, had written something no mother should ever have to write—her son's eulogy. "Tyler was funny, active, excitable, enthusiastic, caring, loyal, curious and loving. His motto in life was simply 'Challenge accepted.'" Jeynelle wrote about her son who had the kindest heart, always telling her he loved her. "At the end of every phone call, every time he left the house and whenever he came home," she said.

Jeynelle said Tyler had referred to himself as Houdini when he was a teenager. But she said it was also true when he was a toddler.

"If you left him alone for five minutes, he would be out the window, up the street in a nappy and a singlet," she said. "Once when I caught up with him, the police had already been called by a concerned passerby and when they asked what he was up to he said, 'I'm catching the bus.'" When Tyler broke his arm on a trampoline he asked his mother to tell his classmates something cooler had happened, like a shark attack. "He was the loudest one in any group, the centre of attention, the one that made everyone laugh. He always had a smile on his face." Jeynelle said Tyler would have done anything for anyone. "He was always there if you needed help—a shoulder to cry on, somebody to lean on. He was your staunchest defender, your strongest ally, and he could make you feel like there was nothing you couldn't face because you had him right by your side."

Tyler's friends were devastated by the loss. Many reached out to Jeynelle and Josh. RIP Tyler was sprayed on the road at the crash scene.

Tyler's close mate Darcy Young cried for hours. Sam Bushby was beyond devastated. He had lost his best mate, the person who had always been there for him in his darkest hours. Sam was at a friend's house when he got the call about the tragedy. He tried to put his phone on charge but the screen went black. Something told him that the call he had just missed was important. He headed home and when he was able to turn on his phone he had about 60 missed calls. When he heard the news, "I looked at my phone, dropped it, and cried my eyes out," Sam said.

Sam didn't know how to cope with the overwhelming grief after Tyler died. "It really destroyed me," Sam said. To add insult to injury he and Tyler had had a falling out before he died. It wasn't the first time they had butted heads and it wouldn't have been the last. But they knew they would soon again be the best of mates. Sadly, Sam would never get the chance to tell his best mate how much he meant to him one last time. "When he passed away I lost my will to live," Sam said. But even in death his mate was there for him. "I had a really bad breakdown and I wanted to kill myself," Sam said. "But that day I felt Tyler there. I felt his hand on my shoulder. I knew it was him. I closed my eyes and I breathed and I calmed down."

Chapter 8

In the weeks and months following Tyler's death, Jeynelle endured the worst pain imaginable. She was stuck on a never-ending rollercoaster of emotions. Sadness, anger, frustration. People tried to be supportive but whenever anyone said "sorry for your loss" she would see red. "I hated it when people said that," she said. "It was the only thing that made me angry. I didn't lose him. He wasn't a set of keys. Someone stole him from me."

Then in what would be the biggest slap in the face since Tyler's death, Jeynelle and Josh found out the man responsible for the death of their beautiful boy was still allowed to drive. He was out on bail and there was no legislation that said someone charged with a hit and run should immediately lose their licence.

One night, when Jeynelle and Josh were on their way to the St Kilda Film Festival, Billy-Jay Glynn drove up next to them. He looked at the couple and he smiled. That was when they knew the man who had taken the life of another felt no remorse. "We couldn't believe it," Jeynelle said. "The fact that he got to keep his licence. You can kill someone with your car and still keep driving."

Determined to see this wrong righted, the couple decided to start a petition calling for a change to the law. All they were asking for was for anyone charged with a hit and run offence to have their licence revoked immediately.

They didn't think it was a big ask. Neither did countless others. "We had so many comments from people saying, 'How isn't this law already?' Most people thought it was."

Jeynelle said car crimes are not being treated seriously enough. "At the moment there is no consequence [until the court process plays out], which is so far down the track," she said. "It makes you feel so powerless that you've lost so much and it is any other day for [the accused]." The online petition was quickly signed by hundreds of the couple's family members and friends. "We're trying to make that change in Tyler's honour," Jeynelle said at the time. "We'd much rather have Tyler with us but we can't, so we're making sure he's not forgotten. We're trying to get something positive out of such a horrible thing and we need as many signatures on it as we can so we the government takes notice." Jeynelle spoke about her bid to change the law on *A Current Affair*.

She said in the days after Tyler's death she hoped he would rush in the front door and tell her it was all a joke. "You don't think about how many photos you've got or how many videos until they're all you've got left." Jeynelle said the last thing Tyler always said as he rushed out the door was "Love ya, Mum." Jeynelle and Josh went to the scene of the accident with the show's film crew. "Just down there," Josh said pointing to the house that Tyler and Oaklee were heading to. "That's where they were going. Half a k [kilometre]… 400 metres." Jeynelle added that they were so close to safety. "It's a trip they had made dozens of times before," she said. "A flat road, straight road. If a car had its headlights on you would see it." Jeynelle expressed on the show her disgust at Glynn's claim that he thought he hit a kangaroo. "I don't know many kangaroos that ride bicycles," she said.

Josh also said he couldn't believe Glynn had kept his licence after that fateful night. "I always thought it would just be one of those things," he said. "You're charged in relation to a hit and run, you would lose or have your licence suspended pending a trial outcome. To me that just seemed like common sense. You wouldn't allow a mass shooter to keep their gun licence and as we've learned a car, much like a gun, can be used as an instrument of death." To not only learn Glynn was still on the road, but watching him drive past them, "I was furious," he said.

Tyler's uncle Christopher Dean was one of the biggest advocates for the petition. "There are lots of ways motorists can lose their licence but hit-run appears to have been overlooked and it must change," he said. "It's not just for our family and what happened, it's just to make a change. It's something that people generally don't think about, that someone can do that and still stay on the road. We think that at least until the case is heard, if the driver has been charged with an offence they shouldn't be on the road." Christopher said seeing the man who had taken her son's life on the road was adding to his sister's grief. "Jeynelle sees him around and it distresses her, she keeps busy... but she sees the guy driving around."

Christopher regrets that he only met his nephew once. But he will never forget it. It was at Jeynelle and Josh's wedding. Christopher was sitting behind Samuel and Tyler. "I said 'Hi' to Samuel, which prompted Tyler to say, 'Who's that?'" He will forever remember the look of excitement on Tyler's face when Samuel told him it was Uncle Christopher. "He stood up immediately and shook my hand and his manners were impeccable," Christopher remembers with a smile.

Josh and Jeynelle set about speaking to politicians about their petition. They were pleased by how receptive ministers such as Jaala Pulford and Luke Donnellan were to their pleas for change. Before they knew it 5000 people had signed the petition. That's when it really gained traction. "It just took off," Jeynelle said. The number of signatures quickly surged to more than 10,000. "Over the months it just kept building." Almost 40,000 people ultimately signed the petition and many shared their own stories of losing a loved one in a hit and run accident and being forced to watch the offender drive on the road.

Senator Derryn Hinch spoke out in support of the push for a change to the law.

"Leaving the scene of an accident, especially a fatal one, is a dog act," Hinch said. "You should not get bail. But if you do, a bail condition must be that you must not get behind the wheel." Hinch said he believed hit and run offenders were one of the most "cowardly, most despicable brands of criminal in this country."

Victorian politician Sarah Henderson also backed the call for a law change. "Subject to exceptional circumstances, there must be a mandatory loss of licence for any person on bail who is accused of a hit-run accident causing death," she said.

Chapter 9

On June 28, 2018, Jeynelle, Josh, and Samuel were forced to come face to face with the man who had ruined their lives. At Glynn's committal hearing in the Geelong Magistrate's Court, the defence argued that Oaklee must have been mistaken when he told police officers the car that hit Tyler did not have its lights on.

Speaking after the court hearing, Jeynelle expressed her sadness at having to relive the horrific events of that October night. "He's killed someone that we loved very, very much," she said. Samuel also spoke, saying he missed the sound of his brother's footsteps running around and hearing about the "crazy things he's done. It's all just a blank space now," he said.

Josh spoke about the push to change the law. "We've seen him [Glynn] on the road many times and we don't think that's acceptable." Ultimately, a date was set for the trial, April 29, 2019. And again Glynn was free to leave the court and drive home if he chose. Expressing her disappointment, Jeynelle wrote on Facebook that by the time of the trial 18 months would have passed since Tyler's death. But the trial was delayed even further and the case didn't begin until June. When it did, Glynn pleaded not guilty to the charges of dangerous driving causing death and failing to render assistance.

The court heard Glynn say he believed he had hit a kangaroo. But Crown Prosecutor

Grant Hayward told jurors it was alleged that
Glynn's vehicle had a faulty alternator at the
time of the accident and it would be argued
that his Nissan Patrol was either travelling
along the road with its headlights turned off or
so dim that they would not have been visible
to Tyler. "It's the prosecution case that Dean
would not and could not have seen the Patrol
coming towards him in time to move out of its
way," Hayward said. He also added that Glynn
should have known the collision had resulted
in a person being killed or seriously injured.
Defence barrister Tim Sullivan denied Glynn's
lights were defective. "The lights were still
effective and they were on," he told the court.

Tyler's friend Oaklee spoke at the hearing,
saying there was "no way" Glynn's car had
lights on. He said the vehicle was driving
"smack bang in the middle of the road"
moments before Tyler was struck. He told the
court the car stopped, turned its lights on, and
drove off, leaving his friend's lifeless body on
the road like a piece of meat. Oaklee told the
court he believed the driver "knew what he

had done," During questioning by Sullivan, Oaklee was asked about the pair's strategy to avoid cars on the road. He was also queried about whether they had smoked marijuana, despite the jury not being told that Glynn, too, had returned a positive test for cannabis on the night in question. Extraordinarily, in a further blow to Tyler's family members in court, Sullivan mistakenly referred to Oaklee as Tyler or Dean on more than one occasion. Oaklee told Sullivan that they used their common sense on the road. "We've done it multiple times," he said. "In the city, may I add, as well."

Oaklee became frustrated at the line of questioning on a number of occasions. When Sullivan asked Oaklee, "You were not in the right head frame, that would be fair to say?" Oaklee quipped back, "A bit like you right now," He also defended himself for not telling police immediately that he didn't have lights on his bike. "No, because it was fucking two hours after the accident. I was on the side of the road," he said. "They wouldn't let me leave the scene. You think I was thinking about fucking whether or not we had lights on our bike?" Sullivan also asked Oaklee whether they had been playing chicken with the oncoming cars. "You might be silly enough to do that, but I'm surely fucking not." He added there was no way Tyler would have been hit if the vehicle's lights were on. "I assure you, if the driver had his headlights on, Tyler would not have been in the middle of the road," he said.

Jeynelle and Josh remember thinking they were facing an uphill battle from day one of the hearing. "At the very start the defence turned around and said to the prosecutor 'I have already agreed on some points so we don't need to bring those up.' They never ever told us what those points were. But the defence wouldn't have agreed to them unless it helped them in some way," Josh said.

They also remember feeling like Tyler was being treated like a number, not the beautiful soul he was. Jeynelle said she introduced herself to Hayward, the man given the task of ensuring justice was served for her son, and was taken aback by his response. "I walked up to him and I said, 'We just want someone who is going to fight for Tyler." She told him she wanted to make sure Tyler wouldn't be treated as a number. "We need someone who is really going to advocate for him," she said. Jeynelle said he fired back at her that he never treated his clients as a number. There were other moments at the hearing that also gave Jeynelle and Josh a sinking feeling about the outcome. There were many details about the night the jury didn't hear, and Glynn's mother wasn't questioned when her story about her son's whereabouts on the day of the accident was different than his girlfriend's account of the day. "The girlfriend said at the committal hearing that he was home all day and that's how she knew he wasn't smoking drugs," Jeynelle said. "Then at the trial his mum said he was at work all day. Where was he? If he was home watching movies he could have been getting his car fixed."

In addition to this, Jeynelle was burning the candle at both ends. During the court hearing she was working nights. "The court obviously didn't know but I was back at work doing night shift so I would finish at 8am, have a quick shower and coffee, and drive to court," she said. "I was exhausted but still got there on time every day."

Chapter 10

In another frustrating moment, Glynn's mother was not pressed in court to explain why she went to the scene of the accident. She was asked if she received a call from her son that night prior to heading to the scene. She replied that she had but was not asked to reveal what was discussed on the call. She told the court she advised her son not to return to the scene of the crime because Oaklee's mother was there. When she returned home, her son was on the verandah. "He was crying," she said. "He was shaking. He was upset. He was—yeah, devastated, basically."

The jury, and Jeynelle and Josh, didn't hear how Glynn supposedly learned he had hit a person. He and his pregnant girlfriend maintained they thought they had hit a kangaroo. Charlotte Manning-Glynn said her partner narrowly missed hitting something—which would have been Oaklee—before he struck Tyler. "Billy then said, 'What the hell?' or something like that and I said to Billy, 'Maybe it was a kangaroo.' Next thing, bang, Billy hit something in the car but I didn't see what it was." She claimed Glynn's headlights were on. The two were returning home to Winchelsea after going to dinner at her grandparents. She said she didn't see anything because she was looking up baby names on her phone. "I just heard like a kangaroo smash, because we hit a kangaroo a week or two prior to this. Just like a bang and then like a… I don't know how to describe it. We just thought it was a kangaroo."

Jeynelle and Josh became hopeful of a guilty verdict when the court was told 23-year-old Glynn told police he had a feeling that he had hit a person. In an interview recorded less than 12 hours after the collision, Glynn said he "saw a glimpse of whiteness" in the seconds before the impact. "I just had that feeling in my gut that it was something other than a kangaroo," Glynn told the officers. He told them that he suggested to Charlotte theyshould return to the scene in case he had hit a person. "The first thing I wanted to do was turn around to see if it was a person but she [Charlotte] was just too upset," he said. That is despite Charlotte telling the court she was "fine because I thought it was a kangaroo."

Jeynelle and Josh wondered how Glynn could be pleading not guilty to the charges of dangerous driving causing death and failing to render assistance when he had admitted to both. In a further ray of hope for the grieving couple, CCTV video of Glynn's car leaving Waurn Ponds Shopping Centre 25 minutes before the accident showed his headlights were not switched on. And in another a-ha moment, Glynn admitted to police his headlights were "pretty shit lately." However, he added he could see fine "like, enough to drive."

Manning-Glynn was asked to explain why she was so upset after the accident if she believed her partner had just hit a kangaroo like he had a week or so before. She was asked why she was crying and shaking and calling her mother-in-law if this was the case. In another move that baffled Jeynelle and Josh, Charlotte was allowed to take a break when she became upset over this line of questioning. "She started crying and the judge turned around said, 'I think we'll break for the day,'" Jeynelle said. Jeynelle and Josh were livid, convinced Manning-Glynn would be coached about how to answer the questions the following day. In addition to that, the judge asked the prosecutor to submit via email the questions he wanted to ask. Jeynelle and Josh admit they are not experts on court proceedings by any means, but this was something they had never heard of happening before. "It's called cross examination for a reason," Jeynelle said. "The next day she [Manning-Glynn] came back dry-eyed and said, 'Nope, it was a kangaroo.'"

Victoria Police mechanical investigation unit officer Brett Gardner examined Glynn's four-wheel-drive. "The bullbar, ah, was distorted," he said. "It had—a—had been impacted on something at some stage." In addition to that he told the court the driving lights fitted on the bullbar were both broken. He said the vehicle's brakes were fully operational, as was the steering system. Senior Constable Gardner said the alternator light came on when he was able to start the vehicle with a slave battery, suggesting the alternator was not working. He was asked whether turning the lights on in a vehicle with a faulty alternator risked draining the battery. He replied that it would. "The longer the lights are turned on the greater the risk of draining the battery?" he was asked. "Yes," replied Senior Constable Gardner, who also said the vehicle's front park lights were not working.

"They were disconnected," he said. "They weren't plugged in." He said that, in addition, the passenger side rear indicator was also not working.

The court also heard from Detective Sergeant Robert Hay, a member of Victoria Police's collision reconstruction and mechanical investigation unit. He said Glynn would have had "almost no chance whatsoever" of seeing Tyler if his headlights weren't working. He also said Tyler would have been able to see Glynn's vehicle if the lights had been switched on. "It creates for him the opportunity to not be in front of the vehicle when it goes past him."

In his final address to the jury, the prosecutor said the claim that Tyler stayed in the path of an oncoming vehicle if its headlights were on did "not make sense. If [Glynn] was shining his lights bright and clear... [Tyler] Dean would have seen him," he said. "He would've moved out of the way and would be alive today."

The jury was then asked to retire to deliberate. It had been a frustrating and trying time for Jeynelle and Josh, who had wanted to scream out several times during the trial the word "objection" or "wait, that's different to what they said last time." But of course they couldn't. Also, there were some details she didn't want to hear. "I left that courtroom every time they talked about injuries or showed photos or anything like that," Jeynelle said. "But Josh didn't. He has things in his head that no one should have to see." Josh said he stayed for Tyler. "I didn't want to give them the satisfaction of leaving too," he said. Josh said there were times when he wanted to stand up and say "fuck this" out of frustration for the lack of empathy for Tyler. He also pictured dragging the driver out of the courtroom and "sorting it out my way." But he wanted to believe "our so-called justice system" would do the right thing.

Josh said he became angry when people would say heartless comments knowing that Jeynelle was in the court. "There were times when his [Glynn's] lawyer would drop a detail such as a quote from a witness like 'No need for an ambulance'… for no other reason than to be petty or officious," Josh said. He said he found the behaviour "childish" and "hateful" and believed the judge should have pulled him up.

Josh said Glynn didn't show any remorse during the court hearing. "He just sat in the dock with a vacant look on his face, almost bored with the whole thing, like we were inconveniencing him in some way," he said. "The only time I recall seeing him emote was the time Jeynelle and I were pulling out to the court carpark after the court had wrapped for the day. He and some of his family members were standing on the corner having a good laugh about something… or someone."

Jeynelle said listening to the testimony was one of the hardest things she had ever done, but she took solace in the fact the case seemed pretty clear cut. "The driver admitted his crime on police video," she said. Jeynelle said Glynn's mother gave a conflicting account of where her son was on the day. In contrast, many witnesses testified that the two boys were in fact doing as Oaklee had said. Jeynelle said, "All the eyewitnesses said the boys were getting well off the road when they saw headlights coming, and Oaklee gave a hysterical first-hand account that the driver did not have lights on within minutes of the crime." In addition to that, police video highlighted all the issues with the car and officers deemed it unroadworthy. Plus, there was that CCTV footage that showed the driver did not have his headlights on at Waurn Ponds. "With all that, how could the jury say he was not guilty when he admitted it himself?"

When the jury retired, Jeynelle and Josh were prepared for a long wait. But it wasn't to be. "The jury took three hours and one was for lunch," Jeynelle said. "We knew it was way too soon." Jeynelle shared her fears with Josh. "I said, 'This isn't good.'" However, she implored Josh and Samuel not to react in any way. "I said, 'Whatever happens, don't give them the satisfaction of showing any emotion. We're just going to hold hands and breathe and see how it goes.'"

In a move that will forever haunt Josh, Jeynelle, and Samuel, the jury found Glynn not guilty on all charges. "It was just rubbish," Jeynelle said. "What keeps going around in my head is if you're sitting in a jury and you hear from enough witnesses that it's dark, you're supposed to believe that he had his headlights on and Tyler just kept riding his bike straight at him. That's what the jury had to believe. No shit, that's what the jury had to believe to find him not guilty of dangerous driving. Because the dangerous driving charge came down to whether he had his headlights on…. This person has killed our son and walked away with nothing and how are we supposed to sleep at night with that?" Jeynelle said the family had had faith in the court process. "That's what happens, right? I can't believe I was so naive." Jeynelle said it was a joke that people could kill someone with their car and their life didn't change. "The victims deserve better," she said.

After the verdict was read, Josh and Jeynelle were delivered another jolt by the prosecutor who had been acting on Tyler's behalf. "He said, 'You can take some solace that he [Glynn] was probably having the worst week of his life.'" How Josh didn't put his hands on the man who had just delivered that low blow, he will never know. It was just another dagger that was wedged into their already shattered hearts.

Jeynelle said that confusion set in in the hours that followed and most days ever since. "I still feel that something went wrong in that courtroom," she said. "I saw a juror listening to private conversations between both families with my own eyes. Another juror admitted that she knew the driver's girlfriend from dance class but was allowed to remain on the jury. The prosecutor got sick and could barely breathe, let alone fight for Tyler. We were cheated."

In the hours that she dissects every moment from that courtroom in her head, Jeynelle wonders whether her resolve to remain stoic throughout the case somehow swayed the jurors to find Glynn not guilty.

Perhaps they felt sorry for the young dad—sympathised with his partner who broke down on the stand. "It always felt like the jury didn't like it that I was strong," she said. "It's like they wanted the show of me sobbing and clutching Josh and falling down. Instead, I was intense. Angry at times, triumphant when witnesses proved our point, flat out tired at other times." She said she fears that the fact she didn't put on a display of a typical grieving mother played some part in the verdict.

78

Chapter 11

The words in the story that was featured in the *Geelong Advertiser* the day after the verdict was handed down said it all. It said the driver who killed Tyler had been cleared of any wrongdoing. It was a bitter pill to swallow. *Cleared of any wrongdoing?* How could that be, Jeynelle wondered. How had the justice system failed her late son so badly? How had the jury come to a consensus on finding Glynn not guilty? Even the judge's closing remarks did little to ease Jeynelle and Josh's pain. "I signalled at the beginning of the trial that this would not bring joy to anyone," Judge Lyon said.

Jeynelle vowed to fight on to change the law that allowed hit and run drivers to continue driving. "Not guilty does not mean innocent," she said. "It just means being a coward with no conscience can be rewarded." Jeynelle said the verdict was proof that car crime was being treated as a joke by the Australian justice system and society as a whole. "When a jury has undeniable proof from the driver himself that he left the scene 'knowing in his gut that he hit a person' and they still say not guilty to failing to render assistance. What can you take from that?" Jeynelle said it was "inexcusable. They will pat themselves on the back for doing their civic duty but won't lose a wink of sleep for the family who has lost their son and has had to watch the killer walk away after confessing on video," she said.

Jeynelle said she had lost faith in the justice system. "I raised my kids to have faith in it and 12 people destroyed that. I will never understand how they got it so wrong." Jeynelle said she feared the jurors had put themselves in Glynn's shoes, not Tyler's. She was also shocked by the attitudes towards car crimes by some on social media. "For every three supportive comments there were three asking what the victim did to cause it," she said. "It became obvious that it came down to some sick popularity contest and once it came out that Tyler smoked marijuana (but the fact the defendant did too was not heard by the jury) the trial was just a one-sided circus." Despite her own losing battle, she vowed to continue to fight for change and to help others who had lost loved ones in similar car crimes.

Josh's mum Di Hayes sat alongside her son and daughter-in-law in court each day. It brought up memories of the teenager she would drop off at school each Wednesday. "I would drop him off and he would be there looking at me, waiting for me to leave," she said. "I would be thinking 'are you going to go to school or not?' I would always wonder whether he did."

Di said Tyler was a "beautiful boy." She said hearing the testimony at the court was traumatic. She said she felt the justice system failed Tyler, her son and her daughter-in-law. "I couldn't believe that he walked free," Di said. "Everyone I talk to is shocked. There is something so wrong with the whole court case." Di said the laws needed to change. "He got less than you get for not obeying the COVID-19 restrictions," she said. Di said it was heartbreaking to sit beside her son and hear all the details of the fateful night. In addition to that, she said Glynn and his family members didn't show a shred of remorse. "No family should have to go through that," she said. Di said she would never have imagined Glynn would be found not guilty on all charges. "I thought he might have got away with dangerous driving but I honestly believed he would be found guilty for leaving the scene," she said. "I was stunned. Absolutely shocked and stunned. Our system is stuffed and that about sums it up." Di said she believed he should have served at least two years in jail. "I still find it very hard to come to terms with," Di said. "Jeynelle has lost a son and Josh has lost a stepson in the worst possible circumstances you could imagine."

Jeynelle's parents Ellen and Laurie Dean supported their daughter and son-in-law from outside the court. They were there to offer a shoulder to lean on, but they didn't want to hear any of the heartbreaking details about how their grandson was taken from them. "We were sitting outside for support," Ellen said. "But I couldn't go into the room itself. I didn't want to hear it."

Ellen said she was devastated beyond belief by the not guilty verdict. "I'm absolutely disgusted by it," she said. "There's something very very wrong with the judicial system. You just have to look at some of the decisions that have been made and you shake your head. He [Glynn] basically admitted it so I don't know how anyone could find him not guilty. He should never have gotten away with it."

Ellen said she and her husband will miss the late night calls from their grandson. "The phone would ring at all hours of the night. It would be Tyler asking if we could pick him up." They never minded getting out of bed. They loved to see their grandson's smiling face and enjoyed listening to him talk about his night out. He would always be surrounded by mates, who they would ensure also got home safe.

Ellen said special occasions would never be the same without Tyler. She said it didn't matter what plans he had, he would always cancel them to spend time with family. "He never left [our] place without a hug," Ellen said. She said she would be eternally grateful to her son-in-law. "Where would our darling daughter Jeynelle be now had she not had you there literally wrapping your arms around her and being such a strong loving support in her darkest hours?" Ellen wrote to Josh on Facebook. "Laurie and I thank you from the bottom of our hearts for all the loving input you put in to help Tyler grow up to be the loveable young lad he became. You were so understanding of him and his ways, which he appreciated very much too." She thanked Josh for helping to ensure Tyler's funeral would be a day to remember. "To just say thank you simply doesn't seem enough," she said. "Please know we are very proud to have you as our son-in-law."

Tyler's uncle Christopher was also devastated by the ruling. "It's cruel that this person took his life from him and there will never be anyone held to account for it," he said. Christopher said he was worried the verdict would set a dangerous precedent. "The not guilty verdict is ludicrous because at the very least he is clearly guilty of hit and run and failing to render assistance. The law has let my nephew down. The law isn't good enough and an inquiry should be held into how many of these cowardly drivers are getting off on technicalities." Christopher said the justice system had "failed dismally. I may have missed out on a lot over many years but when the chips are down I did all I could to help my family. I booked a meeting at the Office of Public Prosecutions in Melbourne to discuss the case and ask why the prosecutor couldn't get a conviction. The prosecutor admitted to me that he failed us."

Christopher said he was disgusted at the other injustices he had read about since Tyler's death. "Virtually all of them get off scot-free, which tells me the law isn't listening," he said. "Accidents happen, I get that, but what happens afterwards is what defines whether we are decent human beings or criminals." Christopher said when a person chooses to leave another person for dead, they should be made to pay. "It's a terrible thing to do and the law is making these criminals feel innocent," he said. "Why?" Christopher said he couldn't understand why there were such inconsistencies in court rulings. "There was a case a few years back when a young man was driving a car with some young girls in the back," he said. The man became distracted by his mobile phone and crashed, killing two of his passengers. "He was jailed for four years because he owned up to his mistake. It didn't help the families of the girls but at least he did the time he was given." Christopher said he didn't know how Tyler's death was much different.

Tyler's close mate Sam Bushby said he had harboured thoughts of taking the law into his own hands following the verdict. "It's fucking disgusting," he said. "The justice system is rigged." Sam said every birthday spent without his best mate by his side was tough. "I miss his smile, especially his cheeky smile when he knew he was right."

On days when Jeynelle and Josh thought their grief couldn't get any worse, they would learn about the horrible things that were being said about Tyler from people close to Glynn. Jeynelle was beyond hurt when a family member of Glynn's wrote on Facebook that people needed to "get over it" and move on. "The family has shown zero remorse," Jeynelle said. "They have laughed at us in town, waved at us, threatened Tyler's friends on Facebook, and now are trolling us on social media. Never once did the driver even quietly say I'm sorry."

In response to Jeynelle's post on the Justice for Tyler Facebook page, Glynn's mother accused Jeynelle of having an overactive imagination. "We are also the ones who have been threatened and have had people try and run us off the road," she said. In a further post she wrote, "And I don't care what you think. Time to move on."

In February 2020, Glynn was back in court. This time it was for returning a positive test for cannabis on the night he hit and killed Tyler. This fact was not included in the prosecution's case against him at trial, despite the fact the defence was allowed to mention and grill Tyler's mate Oaklee about him and Tyler smoking marijuana that day.

The court was told a test taken two hours after the crash revealed Glynn had cannabis in his system. However, he denied that he had been under the influence at the time of the crash, instead saying he'd smoked cannabis when he got home after the incident. His partner Charlotte backed up his claim, saying that he went into shock after learning via a telephone call a person was dead. "He doesn't usually [smoke cannabis] but he was in shock and there was some in the shed, so he went and took some," she said. This was despite the court being told the levels in his system indicated he was a regular user. Glynn's mother also gave evidence, saying he "smoked a few cones" shortly before police arrived to arrest him for his role in the fatal accident.

Josh and Jeynelle had been assured by countless people that justice would be served for Tyler. But when they learned Glynn's punishment for the drug driving offence was a $650 fine and a three-month loss of licence, they realised it was simply another chapter in the nightmare they were living. Especially when they read the magistrate told Glynn the fatal crash was "largely outside of his control" and he hoped he [Glynn] could put it behind him. "How could it be out of his control?" fumed Jeynelle. "He didn't have his headlights on but it was out of his control? He didn't stop to help but it was out of his control? He never apologised but it's out of his control? I don't understand it." Jeynelle shared a post on the Justice for Tyler Facebook page thanking people for their support. "Is $650 enough for the life of my child? Never! But we take comfort where we can and knowing the driver was found guilty."

To add insult to injury, Jeynelle and Josh read about other hit and run accidents in which the offender was sentenced to jail. And while they were happy for the families of the victims, it just reiterated how badly the justice system had failed Tyler. After a crash in Melbourne, Detective Inspector Stuart McGregor was scathing after the person responsible for a hit and run death left the scene. "When they are leaving someone to die, all they are doing is thinking about themselves," he said. "You will get into a hell of a lot more trouble if you leave the scene and not help someone and not call the ambulance." Except if your name was Billy-Jay Glynn, it seemed.

Glynn has never attempted to make amends. Josh said he didn't believe Glynn or any of his family members felt a shred of remorse. "Their behaviour has been nothing but ridicule and contempt and due to the not guilty verdict they clearly feel their behaviour is justified. They've talked themselves into believing it's all on Tyler and Oaklee. Heaven forbid they need to grapple with the concept of responsibility." Josh also said Glynn had hidden behind the cheap shots made about the incident on social media by his family members and friends. "The driver has never said a word. He's happy to hide behind everyone else—the personification of cowardice. Offering an apology would require some brains and some backbone and he, his girlfriend, and their families have shown time and time again they have no stock in either."

Chapter 12

The shock people felt when they learnt that a person who killed another and then left them to die was allowed to keep their licence was evident in the comments section of Jeynelle's petition. Oaklee's mother Melanie Leamer said she was horrified Glynn left Tyler to die and her son alone with only the light of his mobile phone to try to help his mate. "To be able to keep driving around as though nothing has happened is just a kick in the guts to the people whose lives they have destroyed," she said.

One mother sadly knew only too well how Jeynelle felt. Scott Bradley was celebrating his 24th birthday in Mossman, Queensland, on September 3, 2016. He was hit and dragged underneath a car and left to die. His killer, Troy Anthony Salam, pleaded guilty to driving without due care and attention and failing to remain at the scene to render assistance. Shockingly, he never served one day behind bars. Instead, he was given a wholly suspended sentence of six months and lost his licence for a year for fleeing the scene. Scott's mother Janice Bradley launched a campaign for tougher penalties for hit and run drivers in Queensland. She said the state's laws were "weak" and outdated. "If they bring in harsher penalties hopefully some lives can be saved because [the driver] stops to ring Triple Zero and get assistance," Janice said. "Scotty was walking back to where he had been babysitting his friend's two dogs when he was struck and left to die on the road. The person responsible for running over my son travelled 1400 kilometres away after stopping and having his headlight fixed." She said he never served a day in jail despite having four pages of traffic offences, including one charge of causing grievous bodily harm. "I am concerned for other road users," Janice said. "There was no justice for my son. We have now suffered two injustices. The loss of our loveable larrikin, who was loved by everyone who met him, and the fact Salam is still a free man."

Scott and Rachel Bowden also started a petition calling for hit and run laws to be changed in Queensland. Their son Michael, 20, was struck by a vehicle in Weipa in Queensland on June 9, 2018. He was walking home after a night out with friends. "The driver didn't bother to stop, he just went home to bed like it was any other normal day," they wrote in their petition. "Our son was left to die alone in the dark of the night." The man responsible for his death, Vincent Edwards, did not have a licence and it's alleged he was under the influence of drugs. He was sent a notice to appear in court to face driving offence charges, but Michael's parents say that's not good enough. "These men are enjoying their freedom and their lives, while our son lies dead in a lonely grave," they wrote. "We are absolutely devastated, each day for us is a living hell." They have called for a 10-year jail term for people who hit and kill someone and flee the scene.

One person who hopes the person who left him for dead is hit with the full force of the law is James Gilleece. The 21-year-old motorcyclist was driving home to Ararat after visiting Warrnambool about 2.40am on Sunday, January 19, 2020. He estimates he was travelling at about 80km/h through the small town of Bushfield. A vehicle turning onto the highway failed to give way and ploughed into him. James got off his bike and his knees buckled, leaving him lying on the road. "[The man who hit him] parked his car on the side of the road and left it running," James said. "He picked up my bike and moved it off the road but left me lying there." James was shocked when the man quickly got in his car and left the scene when another vehicle pulled up. "He left me on the road and got back in his car," James said. James had blood pouring out of his nose and there was blood on the offender's car. "I'm a very, very lucky boy [to be alive]," he said. James said he supports harsh penalties for people who leave the scene of an accident after injuring someone.

Jeynelle's bid for change was spurred on by the stories that were shared with her as well as her own. "It's not for any form of vengeance," Jeynelle said. "It's for the families that have to put up with these people just driving around." She also started including links on Tyler's Facebook page about instances of car crime. Sadly, this was almost a full-time job, which only further strengthened Jeynelle's resolve.

The Victorian government had made a change to hit and run laws back in 2005 after pressure from the families of two victims. It announced hit and run drivers would face up to 10 years in jail. However, it refused to set a minimum term, instead leaving that to the discretion of courts. At the time Acting Premier John Thwaites said leaving the scene of an accident with the knowledge you have hit someone was a "pretty despicable act. In a case where someone wilfully knows that someone's likely to be injured and they drive off potentially to avoid punishment, a maximum penalty of 10 years is a more appropriate penalty," he said. The announcement came after a teenager in Linton was charged with failing to stop after an accident and failing to render assistance over the hit-run death of 19-year-old Andrew Knowles. Andrew had been walking home from a pub and was only 50 metres from home when he was hit and left for dead. His stepfather, Mick Toleman, found his lifeless body. Toleman said he couldn't understand how anyone could leave someone after hitting them. "You wouldn't leave a dog by the side of the road like that," he said.

Heartbroken mother Julia Donnelly welcomed the change in the law but said the government had taken too long to act. Her son

James, 20, was hit and killed by Phillip Josefski when he was walking home in Canterbury on July 14, 2002. Josefski was sentenced to two years and three months jail.

One of the incidents that sent shockwaves through Australia was when a man ploughed into a man in a wheelchair and then left him for dead. Jake Pedersen, 24, pleaded guilty to hitting Judeland Antony as he attempted to cross Bourke Road in Melbourne on October 30, 2018. Judeland, 33, was thrown from his wheelchair and suffered a broken pelvis, broken hand, and a spinal cord injury. Pederson, a learner driver behind the wheel of a rental car, fled the scene. He denied knowing he had hit a person, but this was refuted. Police prosecutor Sergeant Geoff Adams said CCTV footage of the incident showed Judeland's wheelchair mount the rental car's bonnet in full sight of the driver. In addition to that, Pedersen ran two red lights after the incident and dumped the car. He was sentenced to 40 days in jail and ordered to complete a Community Corrections Order. He was also ordered off the road for 24 months.

Judeland told 3AW's Neil Mitchell he was "sickened" by the sentence. "If he'd never been seen by cameras, he would never have come across and handed himself in," Judeland said. "I'm still going through x-rays, CT scans, and MRIs, and physio, rehab. I still lose balance in my wheelchair and I can't play nationals for wheelchair football." He said the sentence sent a frightening message. "It's not my pain and suffering that's most important, it's the message to the community."

Pederson told the court he was remorseful for his actions and that he had recently relapsed into a meth addiction. Judeland said he didn't think this was any kind of excuse for hitting someone and fleeing the scene. Judeland said he believed Australia's hit and run laws needed to change. He said western countries were often more lenient with penalties, taking into consideration a raft of factors, such as the offender's state of mind and upbringing. "Everyone has a life and difficulties, but you shouldn't be able to say, 'I've had a bad life and that's why I committed a criminal offence. It shouldn't be a green pass."

Judeland, more than anyone, knows what it is like to experience the toughest of challenges life can throw at a person. In his home country of Sri Lanka he was injured in a bomb blast during the ethnic war in 1996. He became a paraplegic.

Judeland does take heart that dozens of people stopped to help him after the hit and run. This is something that doesn't happen in Sri Lanka—people are afraid to get involved. Judeland said he was horrified by the actions of the man who hit him, but he tries to focus on the positives. "There were two different people I was seeing—one person who hit me and ran away and that's sad, that's crazy, that's bad, but on the other side of it there were all these people who stopped to help me."

Judeland suffered a number of fractures, including breaking both hips and further damaging his spine. He said it was difficult to watch footage of the incident. "When I look at the footage of it I just think it's a miracle I'm alive." He regularly endures crippling pain but he hasn't let his latest brush with death affect his zest for life.

On the same program, host Neil Mitchell said hit-run drivers were rarely receiving the maximum penalty of 10 years for their crimes in Victoria, despite crashes critically injuring or killing some victims. In many cases the drivers are slapped with jail sentences under a year, "even after going to extreme lengths to cover up what they did," Mitchell said. He said he had looked into four fatal hit and runs that occurred between 2012 and 2013. "In each case the driver fled the scene and the jail sentence for failing to stop or failing to render assistance was only a few months."

Detective Inspector Bernie Rankin told Mitchell there were four reasons why hit-run drivers flee. "Often they've been involved in a crime prior to the... crash," he said. "[Or] they're either drunk, on drugs, or disqualified from driving. They're the only four reasons why a person who has critically injured someone would contemplate leaving the scene." At the time, Detective Inspector Rankin told Mitchell there were 49 unsolved hit-runs in Victoria dating back to the 1970s.

Colleen Murphy, the grieving daughter of a man hit and left for dead in September 2013, was horrified by the four-month jail sentence her father's killer was given. Thomas Kelly, 80, was hit by a car when he was crossing the road. Peter Chilcott, who was behind the wheel, did not stop. Thomas's body was found on the side of the road 12 hours later. His family will never know if he could have been saved. Colleen said the justice system had let them down. "Our family and friends feel that Dad's life was dishonoured," she told 3AW radio. "It was almost like you lose him twice. You lose him by the horrible circumstances of the crime, the hit-run crime. And then you entrust his life or the care of his life to the criminal justice system and you actually feel like you come away the losers and the perpetrators are the winners because of the lenient sentencing of the court." Murphy said she didn't know how Chilcott and his passenger Lorraine Morris could be so heartless. "I don't ever think I'll understand how they could leave Dad behind at the scene," she said. "They could have phoned anonymously. They were more concerned—and this was on the phone taps—about the fact he [Chilcott] had been drinking and might lose his licence, rather than the loss of my father's life."

At around the same time, *The Age* newspaper reported that every year police in Victoria are tasked to probe up to four serious hit and run collisions. The newspaper shared the stories of four in which the driver had never been charged. In 1996, Patrick Meunier, 19, was living with his family in Melbourne. He had just finished his VCE and was working at Hungry Jack's. On December 20 he was riding his bike to the train station to head to the city for a night out. A witness saw a car driving erratically before it hit Patrick. He was thrown into the air and the driver of the car did not slow down. Detective Inspector Rankin said he couldn't understand how someone could leave another person to die. "When you look at the cold, calculated act of leaving the scene when someone is lying on the side of the road, when prompt medical attention could have saved their lives, it's a despicable thing to do," he said.

In 2012, an elated Jennifer Moller was walking out of the Karingal Bowls Club in Melbourne to greet her husband after winning bingo. She was hit by a car, which was driving erratically. Once again, the driver didn't stop. John Moller had to watch on in horror. "I didn't even see where he came from," he said. "Twenty years of bingo and never a hassle until that day." Police believe they know the man responsible. "Investigators are of the firm view that we are one piece of information away from charging the person responsible," John said. "There's at least three people [involved in the cover-up] and if they told the truth, we'd charge the offender."

In 2005, Luke Shaw was found unconscious with a head wound in Ninth Street, Mildura. The 21-year-old had been drinking at O'Malley's Irish Tavern on October 21. Investigators believe he was either hit by a moving vehicle or fell off the bonnet of a car he may have been sitting on. "Investigators believe there are people in Mildura who have a very good idea of what happened that night," Detective Inspector Rankin said.

In 2007, Mary Firtina was hit by a car on June 19 as she was hit after getting off a bus after a shopping trip. The 73-year-old died in hospital the next day.

But these are just a few of the horrific stories shared in newspapers across Australia. The father of a man who was hit and left for dead while crossing the road in Melbourne in 2017 slammed the sentence his killer was given. Om Paranort, 25, was sentenced to a maximum of three years and nine months for hitting and killing 26-year-old, Damien Cooper. Outside court, Damien's father, Mark, said the result was "disgraceful." He criticised the judge for not slapping Paranort with the maximum sentences for dangerous driving and leaving the scene. "Why didn't he give him 10 years, which is the upper end for leaving the scene? It is not Australian to do something like that and I am absolutely peeved off, and I'll make sure my anger is vented on parliament. It opens the book to all these people out there, hit somebody and rack off. Go away and just leave the scene because you're not going to get anything for it." Mark said he believed the act was "disgraceful" and "non-human. I think any responsible parent will take my view today and think that justice has got to be done and seen to be done, a lot better than it has been."

In July 2015, the man responsible for killing an eight-year-old boy and fleeing the scene was given an 18-month suspended sentence and six months home detention. Matthew Alexander, 23, hit and killed Jack Sultan-Page while Jack was riding his BMX. In sentencing, Justice Stephen Southwood said the offender's conduct had not contributed to the accident, but his failure to stop and assist was "extremely cowardly. Not only did he flee the scene but he parked his car in such a way as to hide the damage," Justice Southwood said. The judge said on the day of the accident the offender's sister witnessed him leaving the house appearing to be "heavily affected" by methamphetamine. He said the role the drugs played in the crash was not known since Alexander fled the scene. Justice Southwood said he took into consideration that Alexander was still a "young man" with a good record and that he had "clearly panicked and fled. Cases such as this are extremely difficult cases," he said. Jack's father Michael Page said his son's death has "wrecked our family completely. We've got nothing," he said. "Our little boy is gone. Never to return. We go and see him every day down the road where he was. Justice should be served."

In March 2018, Maxine Holden crossed double lines and hit 16-year-old Xavier Lengyel, who was riding a motorbike on a rural road in the Northern Territory. Xavier, whose bike was unregistered and didn't have headlights, was left for dead and died from his injuries. Holden told an inquest into his death she didn't render assistance because she "had a really bad headache." She also admitted to washing dye out of her hair moments after the crash. "If you don't rinse hair dye out it gets hot, it can burn your roots," she said.

A grieving mother was horrified when the person who crashed the car in which her son was a passenger was given a $250 fine. Dylan Dahl, 24, was high on ice and ecstasy when he hit a tree near Wollongong in 2016. Jayke Robinson, 18, burned to death when the vehicle burst into flames. Dahl pleaded guilty to negligent driving and speeding at more than 100km/h in an 80km/h zone. However, on the dangerous driving charge he was found not guilty because the judge deemed the poor road conditions and lack of warning signs partly to blame. Dahl was given a $250 fine and a 12-month intensive Community Corrections Order. Jayke's mother Becky was devastated by the ruling. "He took away my son and he just gets a $250 fine—is that all my son's life was worth? Jayke got a death sentence, we all got a life sentence and he [Dahl] walks away scot-free—and he's the one who did all this." Many people shared their feelings about the sentence on social media. "WTF is going on with the judicial system in this country? This is beyond a joke," wrote one. "What an absolute joke.

Something needs to be done with our justice system," wrote another.

Sharon Cuthbert was walking from her car to her front gate in Coolum in Queensland on July 27, 2017 when she was mowed down by a truck driver. A roadside test found Andrew Muirhead had methamphetamine in his system. In addition to this he had a long history of driving offences, according to Sharon's husband Michael. Michael discovered the only reason Muirhead was behind the wheel of a vehicle was because a judge gave him a special licence to allow him to drive for work. He was sentenced to a year in jail and just over a year later was again charged with drug driving. Michael said the lenient sentence "sends no message at all to the public."

In December 2018, just days before Christmas, James Travers was walking home after a night out with mates. Tragically, he was just metres away from his Geelong home when he was hit by a motorist and left for dead. "It was 3 o'clock in the morning, there's a good chance he was out with friends. It's Christmas time, he's done the right thing, he's walking home, he's not driving," a police officer told Seven News. "This person could have stopped and possibly saved his life. I cannot imagine what goes through a person's mind to think it is more important for me to get out of here than saving a person's life." A court was later told the driver who allegedly hit James, Jamie Neskovski, left him for dead and returned to the scene twice but didn't help the dying man. After hitting James, he returned and even shone his headlights on James but didn't get out to help. Detective Senior Constable Ben Oliver told the court nearby CCTV cameras showed James was visible in the van's headlights before the crash. "[Neskovski] turned back towards the collision scene approximately two minutes after the initial impact... and stopped his vehicle for 40 seconds. There is no indication that he got out of the vehicle before he drove off again." The offender eventually handed himself in to police after they released CCTV footage of his van. However, the court was told that police were concerned by the lack of remorse he showed in an interview. In February 2020, Neskovski pleaded not guilty to culpable driving, dangerous driving causing death, failing to stop, failing to render assistance, and a summary charge of careless driving. His sentence, at the time of this writing, is yet to be determined.

In August 2018, New South Wales police announced a $300,000 reward for information on the death of Matthew Mitchell. The 30-year-old was found lying unconscious on the road near Coffs Harbour in August 2013. He died in hospital from serious head injuries. Detective Acting Inspector Peter O'Reilly said he hoped the reward would be the catalyst for someone to come forward about the hit and run death. "It's now been five years since Matthew's death and his family still remain without answers," he said. Matthew's father Peter pleaded for someone to come forward. "If there is anyone out there who was on Graham Drive on the 17th of August and hasn't spoken to police, please tell them what you know so those responsible can be brought to justice," Peter said. "Our son has

died and all we want to know is why. This has
been an incredibly difficult experience for our
family to go through and all we want is some
answers, so please if you know anything that
could help, contact police."

In Darwin in the Northern Territory in
September 2019, Matthew Joseph walked out
of Darwin Local Court with a $1500 fine for a
hit and run incident that left a man with serious
injuries. On March 22, 2019, Joseph struck a
man who was crossing the road, knocking him
off his feet. The man landed on the bonnet
and hit his head on the windscreen before he
was thrown to the ground. A passerby asked
Joseph if he wanted her to call an ambulance.
He said he did and that he needed to move
his car. He then proceeded to flee the scene.
He told his sister about the incident and she
implored him to turn himself in. Despite only
giving Joseph a fine, the judge labelled his
actions as "cowardly."

Jeynelle posted numerous other news
stories in which police were calling for
witnesses to hit and run accidents. Time and

time again police would implore the drivers to come forward.

In November 2019, the heartbroken family of Gladstone's Stephen Moore called for their father's killer to come forward. "We're here today at what we call dad's rock asking for the community's help." Stephen had begun to walk home after his car broke down. He was struck by a vehicle and left for dead. "There is someone that has tragically taken our loved one," his daughter Naomi Barrett said. "If you are this person and listening do the right thing and hand yourself in because we will not stop until justice has been done for our dad."

When Timothy Scollary struck a cyclist while drunk driving near Bendigo in December 2018, the first thing he did was send a text message to his sister. "Call me now. Urgent. Now," he wrote. "I've killed a cyclist. A very good lawyer would be handy." Scollary sent these messages but did not call for help. When police arrived at the scene, he told them he hadn't attempted to render assistance to the victim because he didn't want to "disturb the scene." Scollary was sentenced to three years in jail, with a parole period of 18 months.

Melbourne's Thi Hang Nguyen was spared jail after she hit a 13-year-old cyclist and failed to stop. The girl was left with life-threatening injuries, but survived after she was placed in an induced coma. Nguyen lost her licence for four years and will have to complete 150 hours of community work. County Court Judge Gabrielle Cannon said Nguyen did not attempt to stop and render assistance. "You ought to have known that your crash had caused serious injury," she said. But she also said Nguyen was not responsible for the crash because the cyclist was riding erratically. After the collision, Nguyen fled the scene and dumped her vehicle. Strands of the victim's hair were found on the windscreen. Cycling advocacy group Bicycle Network said Nguyen should have received a jail sentence. "It's a pretty light sentence," the group's chief executive Craig Richards said. He agreed the cyclist was in the wrong but said the judge should have sent a message to the community about the importance of rendering assistance to those hurt in an accident. "We say to everyone 'Please stop, please help if anyone is hurt.'"

In January 2020, Lyn Westeman, a Drysdale woman, was handed a Community Corrections Order and spared time behind bars for crashing into a cyclist, David Clutterbuck. The injuries he suffered left him a quadriplegic. But she attempted to appeal this sentence, which would allow her to remain free unless she breached the terms set out in the order. The initial sentence and the appeal attempt was a slap in the face for the victim. "The person who caused harm to me has been slapped on the back of the hand with a feather," Clutterbuck said.

In March 2020, Mark Lewin was found not guilty of deliberately mowing down two pedestrians on a Geelong footpath. The incident occurred in December 2018. Paula and Christopher Kingscott were walking past a 7-Eleven store when they were hit by Lewin. He fled the scene. Paula suffered a double compound fracture to her lower right leg, while her husband sustained whiplash and body soreness. The couple told a jury they believed they had been struck in a deliberate act. However, Lewin's state of mind at the time of the collision played a central role in his defence. The jury was told he had methadone, nordiazepam, and cannabis in his blood at the time. He was found not guilty of intentionally causing serious injury. The sentence he will receive for pleading guilty to failing to stop and render assistance is yet to be determined.

Like Jeynelle and Josh, Lorraine Gooden is forced to regularly see the person who changed her life forever. The Melbourne woman was left bruised and battered after a woman slammed into her when she was going for her usual daily stroll on May 9, 2019. The driver of the car, Monica Mecham, blew five times over the legal alcohol limit after the crash. Mecham was sentenced to 12 months behind bars after pleading guilty to high-range drink driving. But that was downgraded to a Community Corrections Order and

Mecham is a free woman. In a further chapter to Lorraine's nightmare, she discovered that Mecham's house backs onto hers. Lorraine told *The Daily Mail* it was hard to live so close to the woman who left her with memory loss, a fractured wrist, and facial lacerations. "It's still hard to live here," she said. "For a very long time I was angry about that. Why should we be the ones changing everything about our life and she can just do what she likes?" Lorraine said it was a bitter pill to swallow. "She's the one who's got away with it and we're the ones who feel like we've been prosecuted," she said. Mecham lost her licence for 10 months and Lorraine fears the day she is allowed to return to the road. "My home is my safety net and every time I walk out the door I go 'What if she's driving?' 'What if she's behind me?'"

A Melbourne woman knows she is lucky to be alive after she was hit by a stolen Mercedes and left for dead. Chantelle told *The Age* she was cycling along Chapel Street in Melbourne in May 2020 when a white Mercedes veered into the bike lane and hit her. Chantelle was thrown onto the bonnet of the car and then fell on the road. CCTV footage shows the driver did a U-turn and drove off after hitting her. "I remember looking up from the ground because I wasn't able to move, saw the car stop and do a U-turn and then drive straight back past me," she said. Chantelle said she was lucky she didn't land on her head. She was shocked when she viewed the footage of the incident. "I didn't realise that I'd actually hit the bonnet until I've seen some footage," she said. "It was actually really difficult to watch the footage, to bring back the memories of the trauma. But also, it brought back the memories and the feelings I had at the time of the accident, which was 'How the hell can someone actually leave when you could be dead on the side of the road?'" Chantelle said there was no doubt in her mind that the person knew they had hit her. Luckily, another motorist came to her aid. Sergeant Lachlan Dunlop said it was a despicable act to leave the scene of a crash. "I'm not sure where the conscience is of someone who can do that to another human," he said.

In May 2020, Deborah Locco, 60, was cycling along Beach Road in Melbourne. It was a regular weekend bike ride for the former school principal. She was wearing reflective gear, had lights on her bike, and was cycling in the bike lane when she was struck from behind by Christopher Hislop, 35. He fled the scene and later dumped the car he was driving. "I still can't get my head around why you don't stop," Detective Sergeant Mark Amos said after the incident. "There is no reason, there is no excuse." Witnesses said they saw Hislop's car driving erratically in the moments leading up to the crash. He has been charged with culpable driving, dangerous driving causing death, failing to stop, and failing to render assistance. He has yet to face court on these charges.

Other cases where the offenders pleaded guilty and tougher sentences were handed down brought up mixed feelings for Jeynelle and Josh. They were pleased other families were given some sort of justice, but it also made them wonder why their outcome had been so very different. "All these people are pleading guilty and taking at least a minor punishment," Jeynelle wrote on the Justice for Tyler Facebook page. "The gutless coward in our case didn't even have the guts to do that and was rewarded by the jury."

Hit and run laws have been called into question all over the world, not just in Australia. A petition launched by the parents of New Zealand's Nathan Kraatskow calling for tougher sentences was signed by 280,000 people. "Our 15-year-old son Nathan was killed in a hit and run and the 19-year-old girl that killed him under the influence of drugs and alcohol only got 11 months home detention," Charlene Kraatskow wrote. "What about my son and where is the justice here?" Nathan was cycling home from a mate's place in May 2018 when he was knocked off his bike by Rouxie Le Roux. She was on a learner licence and had been drinking wine and smoking cannabis before getting behind the wheel of her friend's Mercedes Benz. She fled the scene. Nathan's father Orion said he doesn't believe Le Roux has been adequately punished for killing and abandoning his son. "She doesn't deserve a second chance," he told the *Otago Daily Times*. "She hasn't shown remorse that we've seen. She has had it so easy, she hasn't had a punishment. Imprisonment was justifiable. We feel we are being walked over and she is getting whatever she wants." In a further slap in the face to the family, Le Roux posted photos of her on a beach during home detention. "It's called 'unspecified time' where I was allowed to have four hours out of the house. That happened near the end of my sentence," she said. Orion and his wife spoke to politicians and called for tougher home detention conditions. They asked for limited access to television and social media. "It's a holiday house," they said of home detention.

In Missouri in the United States, Stacey Stevens started a petition calling for tougher hit and run laws. "On September 12, 2015, my 19-year-old son Matthew Brooks Stevens was walking along Highway 59 in Neosho, MO, when he was hit and killed," she wrote.

"The man who hit my son left him for dead in the middle of the highway and fled the scene." She said it wasn't until two weeks later that he, flanked by an attorney, handed himself in. "In the state of Missouri, if you leave the scene of an accident, the maximum sentence is a felony which carries a sentence of four years in prison and a $5000 fine. That's it." She said the driver would not have his licence suspended or revoked. "Please help me send a clear message to our legislators that our loved ones are more valuable than a $5000 fine," she said. Her petition has been signed by 139,000 people.

Meanwhile, in Chicago, IL, the family of a 13-year-old cyclist, Isaac Martinez, killed in a hit and run accident in July 2020 is outraged the judge set the alleged offender's bond at $50,000. His mother Itzl Dirzo said, "I want justice for my son because it's not fair that he's getting out with a bail bond." Isaac was riding his bike to his cousin's house when he was struck. Investigators say Oscar Martinez Guerrero did not stop or call for assistance after hitting Isaac.

In the UK, there was a call to increase the penalties for hit and run drivers after the deaths of Zaneta Krokova, 11, and Helena Kotlorova, 12, on New Year's Eve in 2016. Gabor Hegedus, 38, hit the two cousins as they crossed the road hand in hand. He was sentenced to four years jail after pleading guilty to causing death by careless driving, failing to stop after a collision, failing to report a collision, driving without a licence, and conspiracy to pervert the course of justice. A petition labelled the sentence "disgraceful. It makes my blood boil," it states. "How do you get just four years for taking the lives of two innocent children? Has the justice system worked here? Is this really the world we live in?" The petition called for tougher laws. "The maximum prison sentence for causing death by careless or inconsiderate driving is five years; and for causing death whilst driving unlicenced, disqualified, or uninsured it is two years. How does this sentence deter others from putting people's lives in serious danger?" The petition calls for the laws to be reviewed. "We need to address and change the laws written for dangerous driving or careless driving immediately," it states. "We need to review the sentencing to prevent families from having their world ripped apart. No human being should be allowed to walk the streets and get behind the wheel of a car again in such a pitifully short space of time after committing such a horrendous crime."

Patricia Arnold signed the petition, saying she fully supported a review of the laws. "My brother was 19 when he was killed by a driver who was drunk and on drugs," she wrote. "The driver fled the scene. The next day he tried to scrap the car and went into hiding. When he was found all he got was a six-week sentence, which was an absolute insult to my family. And his son was a baby. Six weeks for a life."

In Canada, Kerry Nevin called for a court ruling to be appealed after the man who killed his son in a hit and run accident was spared jail time. Deinsberg St-Hilaire was ordered to complete community service and stick to a curfew after he was found guilty of attempting to cover up the incident. St-Hilaire said he was asleep when he struck Andy Nevin in south Ottawa on June 28, 2015. He said he woke up and heard a bang and thought he had hit a mailbox. He was found not guilty of dangerous driving causing death and failing to remain at the scene. Andy's family labelled the sentence "sickening" as they walked out of the court. Nadia Robinson, Nevin's former partner and the mother of his two sons, expressed her frustration at the sentence. "He [St-Hilaire] gets a slap on the wrist," she said. "They're not setting a good example for future cases, that's for sure. I don't agree with the judge. He should have done at least some time. I knew we weren't going to get a lot, but some time…. Andy's not here to help support my kids." The family's push for an appeal was rejected.

Chapter 13

Gavin and Shona Potter know only too well how it feels to be let down by the justice system. Their son Preston Potter was the victim of a hit and run on June 6, 2019. The 16-year-old had been hanging out with two mates on the Gold Coast in Queensland. They were celebrating the fact they had completed TAFE certificates to allow them to pursue an apprenticeship in their chosen trades.

Preston wanted to be a plumber. "He asked if he could go to his mate's grandmother's house and celebrate," Shona said. "He asked if he could go and play pool, watch Netflix, and have a couple of beers," she said. Preston had completed a plumbing certificate and had an interview for an apprenticeship lined up the following day. It was an appointment he would never attend. Instead, he would be in a coma struggling for his life.

Shona said the mates decided they wanted something to eat and decided to go for a walk to a nearby service station to get some Subway. "They didn't want to ask her to cook," Shona said. The three attempted to cross Bermuda Street in Burleigh Waters. A speeding car, which onlookers said had a clear view of the road in front of it, hit Preston.

Witnesses later said he was thrown metres up into the air. In a move that shocked everyone at the scene, the driver of the vehicle kept driving. Luckily for Preston, a trainee nurse at the scene immediately sprung into action. She administered CPR and most certainly saved his life, Shona said. Gavin describes the nurse as an "angel." An ambulance was called and paramedics worked for hours at the scene to stabilise him. If they hadn't, he would have certainly died en route to hospital.

Shona and Gavin were told to head to the hospital immediately. But when they arrived, a social worker told them it was probably better if they didn't see their son because it was unlikely they would recognise him due to his injuries. Preston's parents were told to prepare for the worst. He had suffered serious injuries including a skull fracture. He was placed in an induced coma, which he remained in for eight days.

On June 9, Gavin created the Facebook page Pray for Preston. The response and outpouring of emotion was overwhelming. Thousands of people sent messages of support, assuring the family that Preston was in their prayers. Gavin vowed to keep followers of the page informed about his son's progress.

On June 11, he sadly shared that Preston had experienced a setback. "He was supposed to start to be woken up and they could [not] because of complications," Gavin wrote. He added that doctors had grave concerns about Preston's progress because of blood flow in his brain. "We are scared and anxious," he wrote. He added that the two were stuck on a rollercoaster of emotions—of hope, fear, and anger after learning the cause of their son's fight for his life. However, Gavin added, "we are overwhelmed with the love that is being shared." In addition to a serious brain injury, Preston suffered a horrific break to his leg and had to have plates and screws placed in it.

Preston's mates at his under 16 football team the Parkwood Sharks wore armbands and marked a moment's silence for their mate. "Keep fighting champion," one person wrote on the Pray for Preston Facebook page.

On June 15, an elated Gavin posted that Preston had begun to breathe on his own. "This was by far the best birthday present for Shona," he wrote. "We were beside ourselves with joy. One small step but obviously amazing." Gavin further added that Preston had moved his left arm occasionally.

A friend of the family, Budd Seeto, began a GoFundMe page for Preston. "Preston Potter is currently in intensive care after being the victim of a cowardly hit and run," he wrote. "He has injuries to his brain and some badly broken bones, which will make for a long recovery. The aim of this fundraiser is to help give the parents Gavin and Shona the best medical care and rehabilitation available and the remainder—if any—can go to Preston. Even the smallest amount can make a difference so please help with what you can." Friends and family members and people who didn't even know them quickly dug deep and the amount surpassed $10,000 Aus in a short period of time.

Meanwhile, Gavin and Shona kept vigil at their son's bedside. "We just stayed with him and prayed," Shona said. She admits she is not a religious person, but she was going to do everything in her power to bring her son back.

On June 14, doctors began to bring Preston out of the induced coma. "No response yet but we hope in the coming days he will start to respond," Gavin shared on Facebook. Then in a moment that made Gavin and Shona realise their prayers were being heard, their son filled them with hope. On June 17, Preston opened his eyes for the first time. "Today our son opened his eyes and looked at us both," Gavin said.

Seeto addressed the media about Preston and said his parents were remaining positive. He also said they wanted him to urge people to take care on the roads. "They want to tell people to be safer on the roads, for young people to take extra care as they are the most precious things in their family."

Gavin and Shona then learned the driver of the car, Robert Summerville, 44, had failed a drug test. Not only had he hit Preston and fled the scene, he was high on ice and driving an unregistered vehicle. It was also revealed that it was not his first drug driving offence. In a further blow—and one that seemed incredulous—the man had his licence suspended for 24 hours after he was charged and after that he was allowed to return behind the wheel.

Shona now knows that her son came scarily close to crossing over. "He does remember going to heaven when he was in ICU," she said. "He remembers seeing my dad. He said 'I saw Poppy and Poppy was angry I was there. He told me You can't be here, mate.' He has very vividly described seeing a whole bunch of people," Shona said.

Preston has continued to amaze doctors and his family with his recovery. But his life has been forever changed. He has a global brain injury and is not the same person he once was. He most likely won't be able to pursue his desire to become a plumber. His mother Shona said he suffers with anger issues, had blurred vision for months, lost hearing in one ear, and his shattered leg will never be the same. He often asks his mother, "Why did this happen, Mum?" It's a question she can't answer.

In the months that followed the accident, police assured the family they would be given the chance to write and read victim impact statements when the driver faced court. But in a move that Shona says is beyond belief and unforgivable, they were not informed that Summerville was appearing in court. "The media called us and said we've just been advised by Queensland Police Service that the court case was this morning," Shona said. She wondered if she was the victim of some sick joke when she was told that the driver had received a $500 fine. The man who struck her son, sending him flying metres into the air, and callously left the scene had walked free from court with a $500 fine and a one month loss of licence. High on ice, driving an unregistered vehicle, he had left Preston for dead and was hit with a penalty that is less than what a person who uses their mobile phone while driving receives. Shona was devastated. "I was crying and I was saying 'That's unacceptable.'" And not only was the pathetic sentence a slap in the face, their promise of having their say in court had not been kept. "I'll never understand or be able to fathom why these crime laws are so f--king inadequate and how little human life is worth," she said.

Shona and Gavin decided to fight for a tougher penalty, a change to the law and for—at the very least—an apology from the Queensland Police Service that they were not informed about the court hearing.

Shona said she had since learned that car crime laws in Australia were in desperate need of reform. "Unfortunately the whole of Australia needs an upheaval with car crime laws,." Thousands of Queenslanders expressed anger when they heard news of the $500 fine. Queensland politician Sam O'Connor was one of the people the family contacted for help. Like them he was outraged by the miscarriage of justice. He vowed to advocate for change and helped them launch a petition calling on the state's premier to appeal the driver's sentence and to review the laws.

Gavin spoke to radio presenter Luke Bona about the pathetic sentence. Bona, like so many others, could not believe what he was hearing. He told his listeners the sentence had been labelled "unjust" and "disgraceful," and he concluded it didn't "pass the pub test." He said it sent the wrong message. Gavin told Luke he and his wife were thankful every single day that Preston had survived, but lamented the incident was "totally avoidable" and "should never have happened." He said the couple never expected such a shocking outcome. "It's unbelievable," Bona said. He added that the driver had received a fine that was half as much as a Queensland driver would be hit with if they were caught using a mobile phone. "It's just outrageous," he said. Gavin told Bona witnesses to the crash said it didn't appear the driver of the vehicle made any attempt to slow down at the intersection. Gavin said his son's life was forever changed. "He's 16 years old and he had the world in his hands." Bona said he was sure all of his listeners were shaking their heads in disbelief. Close to 10,000 signed a petition calling for the penalty for the driver to be upgraded.

Shona said when she asked for answers about the ruling, she was told three words that she hopes she never hears again. Those words were "It's within range." Words that make her blood boil. "Please feel free to share your concerns with our heads of government," she wrote on the Pray for Preston page. "I have to believe we have left no stone unturned. The outcome so far has been 'It's within range.'" Shona said car crime laws across Australia were inconsistent and inadequate. "It's very upsetting to know how different the outcomes can be," she said. "It depends on the investigation and who you have as a judge. It's absolutely disgusting to think that a human being can be treated this way."

Politician Sam O'Connor sent the petition to Queensland Premier Annastacia Palaszczuk and spoke about the issue in parliament. He said he was shocked the penalty imposed to the hit and run driver "nowhere near" matched the crime. O'Connor told his fellow members of parliament that Preston, a youngster who loved footy and was a role model to his two younger sisters, was "struck down by a driver high on ice." In addition, the driver was speeding and driving an unregistered car and drove off, leaving Preston for dead on the side of the road. What sort of punishment would the driver receive, he asked his fellow politicians. He revealed, to sounds of shock, that the driver was hit with a $500 fine and again repeated the fact: This is half the penalty for using a mobile phone while driving. "The Potter family and my community are angry," Mr O'Connor said. "Their hearts are broken by this soft sentence. All the Potters want is for the punishment to fit the crime. They deserve justice for everything their son has lost."

Sadly, the Potter family was forced to abandon their bid to appeal the penalty handed down when Preston suffered a seizure. There was still much to be done with regard to the appeal, but Shona and Gavin had to prioritise caring for their son. Despite this, Shona has vowed to continue to fight for changes to the pathetic car crime laws. "We're very blessed to still have him," she said. "If he's happy, I'm happy and he's in a good place. But I will continue to push for change."

Shona said her husband had been promised by politician David Janetzki he would push for changes to the laws if he was elected. And they plan to hold him to it. "He promised that if he's in power he will review the laws immediately," Shona said. "He looked Gavin in the eye and said 'I know it's deplorable.'" The two hope that day will come. And they pray it's sooner rather than later because they don't want any other family to endure what they have.

In January 2019, Mr Janetzki announced he would push for changes to hit and run laws. He called for an increase in penalties for hit and run drivers. "The laws dealing with hit and run offences are clearly inadequate and Queenslanders are demanding change," he said. "We believe hit and run offenders who callously flee the scene should spend time behind bars." He said the maximum penalty in Queensland was three years jail, while most other states had a minimum of five to 10 years. "Callous hit and run offenders are receiving a slap on the wrist or in other words a 'wholly suspended sentence' and frankly this is not good enough. We are calling on the

Palaszczuk Government to review the current law and bring Queensland penalties into line with other states." Mr Janetzki said families of hit and run victims were suffering enough and needed to know that their loved one's life was properly valued by the law. "Knowingly fleeing an accident and leaving an injured or dead person behind is a despicable act and offenders should be held accountable."

Chapter 14

In South Australia, a family has launched a campaign calling for tougher penalties for drivers who cause fatal crashes. Luke Dobbins was riding his motorbike on June 22, 2019 when a ute pulled out in front of him. The 22-year-old was thrown from his bike and hit by a second car. He died at the scene. The man responsible for his death, Jack McDonald, was handed a three-month suspended jail sentence and a $5000 two-year bond. Luke's parents Keith and Veronica are shocked by the lenient sentence. During the sentencing process, they spent $10,000 to erect a billboard outside the Mount Gambier court calling for tougher penalties. Keith and Veronica have asked people to contact politicians to call for change. Keith believes tougher penalties will act as a deterrent. "They keep talking about lowering the road toll but they won't back it up in court," Keith said.

Another family fighting for justice is the Little family. Lee Little is doing everything in her power to fight for changes to car crime laws and domestic violence laws. On December 28, 2017, Alicia Little was mowed down with a Toyota Hilux by her partner Charles McKenzie Ross Evans at the couple's Kyneton home. The 41-year-old was struck by the front driver's side of Evans' vehicle as he drove between a water tank and fence at between 12 and 16km/h. Instead of assisting his partner, he fled the scene. Shortly before the accident, Alicia had called Triple-0. She said Evans was drunk and being abusive. But when officers arrived 16 minutes later, Alicia was dead.

Evans pleaded guilty to dangerous driving causing death and failing to render assistance. The initial charge of murder was downgraded, much to the disbelief of Alicia's family. They were even more shocked to learn his sentence was a maximum four years in jail with a non-parole period of two-and-a-half years.

Lee said her daughter had suffered years of violence at the hands of Evans. Sadly, her daughter's forgiving nature meant she believed him when he apologised and promised he would change.

"She was so full of life," Lee said. "She would light up a room. Sadly, her biggest downfall was that she wanted to repair people. She wanted to help everyone. As a kid she used to bring homeless kids home all the time. She would ask, 'Mum, can they stay for dinner? Mum can they stay the night?'" It was this pure heart and empathy that allowed Evans to prey on her daughter, Lee said. She wants changes to car crime laws and also wants a national database of domestic violence offenders. This, she believes, would help people like her daughter avoid finding themselves in a relationship with a violent perpetrator they can't escape.

Lee is sad that she couldn't convince her daughter to stay away from Evans after the first time he physically assaulted her. "The first time he bashed her she came home," Lee said. She was relieved to hear her daughter say she would never return. But Evans was calculating and manipulative—he knew how to appeal to Alicia's kind heart. "She had nothing to do with him, she had blocked him so he couldn't contact her," Lee said. But that didn't stop Evans. He asked a family member to get back in touch with Alicia. And sadly, she was drawn back in by his promises of change, his grovelling apology. "He promised he was getting help and it would never happen again." Lee feared this would be short lived, and she was right.

When Alicia missed Christmas, Lee knew something wasn't right. "She never missed

Christmas," Lee said. "We have about 130 people every year and when she didn't come I knew there was something wrong."

Lee said Evans controlled every aspect of her daughter's life. He didn't like her four children being around because he got jealous she was not giving him her full attention. "He wanted to know where she was at all times," Lee said. She recalls one horrific night in particular. "I remember one time he put her in the hospital I was on the phone to her when he came home," she said. "He said to her, 'Who the f are you talking to!?' and she said 'I'm talking to my mum.'" Shockingly, Lee then heard a confrontation and the phone thrown down. She listened—terrified—as he threw her to the ground and told her she was "better off dead."

The couple announced their engagement two weeks before Alicia's death, but Lee knew all was not well. She chokes back tears when she remembers a conversation she had with her daughter. "I sent Alicia an email," Lee said. "It was a poem about mothers and I rang Alicia and asked her if she got it." Lee's daughter told her she had not. She said that Evans had deleted all her emails and all the contacts in her phone. He had also deleted all of her family photos. "She said, 'The only phone number I have is yours, which I know off by heart.'" Lee said her daughter had to hide in the shower or go for a walk to talk to her.

On the day she died, Alicia told her mother she was going to leave. It's for this reason Lee believes her daughter was murdered. Further evidence of this, she says, is that Alicia's car had been immobilised. Lee believes this was done to prevent Alicia from leaving. The last text message Lee received from her daughter chillingly said: "In the next 24 hours there is going to be drama."

In what seemed more like a nightmare than real life, Lee learnt of the incident on the news. "I had the 5 o'clock news on and then it came over the news and I knew her car and I knew it was her," Lee said.

When she heard the man who had killed her beautiful daughter may only serve two and a half years for his crime, her legs buckled. "I went to my knees and cried. I couldn't believe that's all my daughter's life was worth. It's wrecked us."

Alicia's close friend Mel Sell said the pathetic sentence was infuriating. "It's very angering to know he received a higher driving disqualification [five years] than he did a jail sentence for killing her," she said. Alicia's brother Bronson Little branded the sentence "absolutely ridiculous. Where's the justice?" he said. "I don't know what's wrong with our justice system but it needs to be fixed. If we can save one person out of this, we will feel like we have achieved something."

Alicia's aunt Cindy Miller launched a petition calling for tougher sentences. "My beautiful niece Alicia Little was run over and left to die by her abusive fiancé," she wrote. "Our family is devastated to have lost a precious daughter, niece, sister, aunt, and loving mother of four. He left Alicia lying there, bleeding and suffering in pain." He did not bother giving her any assistance or calling an ambulance. "Alicia died that day because of the brutal way in which Charlie Evans inflicted injuries on her." Cindy also said Evans was sentenced to just four years for his "cruel and cowardly act. His charges were downgraded to dangerous driving and failure to render assistance because of a plea deal. I feel very let down by our justice system. Is Alicia's life worth just four years? My niece deserves justice."

When Evans' sentence was handed down, Alicia's sister-in-law Lauren Little addressed the media outside of court. "Alicia was a fun, charismatic, adventurous spirit who had an unimaginable ability for human compassion," she said. "She died alone and her injuries were so severe they could no longer support life. This was done by someone who only weeks before had asked for permission to marry her."

Lee said no amount of time or penalty would reverse the outcome for their loved one. "We will all be forever changed because of this completely unnecessary loss of life," she said. "Her four children have been stripped of sharing a future with her. They will go on without their mother enjoying many of the milestones that she had so fondly talked to them about. The void of her loss will continue to be deep and overwhelming." Lee said there needed to be changes to the justice system. "We need people to get noisy about this." More than 45,000 people have signed the petition calling for a national database of domestic violence offenders. However, Evans may be released any day on parole. "He's going to be out and I'm scared he's going to do it to someone else," Lee Little said of Evans' looming release.

Chapter 15

The knowledge that other people had been successful in changing laws regarding car crime helped Jeynelle and Josh in their tough days of fighting on behalf of Tyler. Kevin Saul successfully changed hit and run legislation in New South Wales after his nine-year-old son was killed by an unlicenced driver in Dubbo in January 2004. The youth who hit and killed Brendan Saul while he was riding his bike with his 11-year-old brother Matthew had drugs in his system. Shockingly, the charges against the youth, who has never expressed any remorse or apologised to the family, were thrown out of court. Kevin was livid and shocked by the ruling. "You try to teach kids right and wrong," he said. "Not to take drugs, not to drive a car if they shouldn't be—and now we're told it's wrong but not against the law. This is not a justice system, it's a legal system. If you're young, if you lie, if you run, if you hide, you get away with it." The youth had taken morphine and cannabis before getting behind the wheel that fateful day.

Kevin remembers police officers arriving at his work after the accident. "They said 'Come with me' and I don't argue with men with guns," he said. He didn't realise something was terribly wrong until he noticed they were heading in the direction of the hospital. Initially the parents were told their son would be transported to Sydney. But they were later advised his injuries were too great and he wouldn't survive.

The heartbroken family was convinced they would see some sort of justice for their son. But that wasn't to be. Kevin said the magistrate reasoned that there wasn't enough evidence to prove the youth had been driving in a dangerous manner at the point of impact. Apparently—and incredulously—the fact he was unlicenced and driving while under the influence of drugs wasn't enough to prove this charge.

Kevin vowed to push for change for Brendan. He also wanted changes to the legal system that he said was skewed against victims. Because the offender was a minor, Kevin had to ask permission from the defendant's solicitor to be allowed to observe the court proceedings. "For the first two weeks I had to ask permission to go into the court each day," he said. Since the offender gave permission, it was eventually noted that he no longer had to ask. But it was still a slap in the face for the grieving father. Kevin said he never thought he would be responsible for helping to change a law. "Basically, I just had the shits and wanted to change it," he said.

Kevin was also livid when it was revealed the youth responsible for his son's death had got his hands on autopsy photos and bragged about them. He found out that under NSW law juveniles were allowed to access the brief about their case. Kevin was not. In NSW parliament in February 2005, Nationals' leader Andrew Stoner asked why this had occurred. "Why is the juvenile system so out of control that you allowed the 17-year-old driver responsible for the death of nine-year-old Brendan Saul to get hold of autopsy photos of the victim, show them to his mates, and get high fives from his mates after the acquittal?"

Politician Diane Beamer was a great help in pushing for change, Kevin said. And in September 2005, Brendan's Law was read in parliament for the first time. Ms Beamer said the bill would see heavier penalties for people who failed to stop after hitting someone with a car. She said the changes were being introduced in "recognition of society's abhorrence of those who injure their fellow citizens and then abandon them to die. When a driver leaves the scene of an accident, leaving in his or her wake a dead or badly injured person without attempting to render assistance, the fundamental code of civilised society is breached," Ms Beamer said. "Every driver on our roads needs to be aware that with the privilege of driving on our roads comes a fundamental responsibility to our fellow drivers." She said under the changes, the maximum penalty for failing to stop after a hit and run accident would be 10 years. "When the collision causes grievous bodily harm, the maximum penalty for failure to stop is [currently] seven years," she said. Ms Beamer said the law would apply to any person who gets behind a wheel, irrespective of age or whether they have a licence. "The focus of the new offences is to ensure assistance for victims of serious vehicle impacts," she said. "Assistance may save a life, minimise injury, improve the prospect of recovery, alleviate suffering, and preserve the dignity of the injured or deceased." Beamer said failure to stop and render assistance should "invite significant punishment."

Kevin said he was pleased he had achieved change for "Brendy" but he believes educating drivers about the possible ramifications of their actions is even more important. He has spent hours talking to people who have been charged with a driving offence about what happened to his son. "I would talk about Brendan's accident and how it affected our family. People need to realise that a vehicle is a two tonne weapon," he said. His three living sons haven't ridden a bike since that tragic day and each was reluctant to obtain their driver's licences.

Kevin has been approached by a number of people who told him his speech helped them turn their lives around, when they had previously taken little care on the roads and often got behind the wheel intoxicated. Kevin said that was Brendan's legacy. "When that happens I think 'we've done something good for Brendan.'" He is relieved NSW's car crime laws now are "far better" than that in any other Australian state. "The other state's laws are shit," he said. "We should have a federal law for driving." Kevin is proud that Brendan's law is unique. "It's the only law in the Westminster system where you have to prove your innocence. Under the law if you're driving you are guilty until you can prove you are innocent."

Kevin said another positive he took away from the tragedy was the fact he lived in such a supportive community. "From the first moment when dealing with the police, ambos, doctors, and nurses, each of them felt our pain and grief. Our greatest strength is the way everyone in town rallies around one of our own, or not even our own, when something tragic happens. People dig deep, real deep to find that special something that is needed and nothing, I mean nothing, is too much trouble."

Kevin said he believed his son would have been a talented rugby player like his brothers. He thinks of him often with a smile on his face.

Chapter 16

On Tuesday, November 26, 2019, as a result of Jeynelle's efforts, the Road Safety and Other Legislation bill 2019 was introduced to Victorian parliament for the first time. Police and Emergency Services Minister Lisa Neville said the bill aimed to improve road safety by introducing immediate suspension of licences to apply to excessive speeding offences and when a person uses a motor vehicle as a weapon in the commission of serious offences. "These changes support the rights of victims and families of victims who have died or suffered serious harm to their physical or mental health as a result of dangerous drivers," Ms Neville said. "They also align with community expectations that licence suspension should be an outcome of being charged with serious driving offences because there is a clear risk to public safety." Lisa said the changes were largely a result of the actions of Jeynelle and Chloe Dickman, who was the victim of a horrific motor vehicle assault on July 25, 2015. The bill states that Victoria Police will now have the power to suspend a person's licence in circumstances where a person uses a motor vehicle to commit a serious offence such as murder, attempted murder, or causing serious injury either intentionally or recklessly. When talking about the bill, politician Ed O'Donohue said Jeynelle perfectly captured why the law should be changed when she said "if you shoot someone with a gun, they lose the gun. If you stab someone with a knife, you lose the knife… but they can hit someone with their car, kill them, and just keep driving like it doesn't mean a thing." He applauded her for vowing to fight to make people realise cars were weapons. "I will fight to make changes and try to change the way society thinks about car crime," Jeynelle said.

Mr O'Donohue said it was regrettable that it sometimes took a tragedy for the community to realise there was a deficiency in a law. "It is unfortunate that often the law is reacting to things that have occurred that are manifestly incorrect and manifestly out of touch with the expectations of the community and it takes that tragedy to drive legislative change to close a loophole, to make it stricter, tighter, and to deliver a message of deterrence that that sort of behaviour is not acceptable," he said.

Tania Maxwell, another Victorian politician, said she hoped Jeynelle's message would be shared far and wide "so that others driving a motor vehicle will be responsible and think about how their lives can be changed in an instant." She spoke in support of the bill, saying the changes were urgently needed. She said Jeynelle and Josh had endured extraordinary heartbreak since Tyler's death. "They have been through so much, including two exhausting court cases, yet they have never given up," she said. Maxwell said she sincerely hoped the bill would reduce the number of hit and run incidents in Victoria. "Hit and run driving is a truly sickening and, unfortunately, all too prevalent crime," she said. "In fact, I will borrow from the words of [Senator] Derryn Hinch himself to say that the instigators of hit and run accidents are cowards whose lack of compassion towards their victims is despicable." Tania said police records revealed there were nearly 150 deaths and more than 18,000 injuries from hit and run driving in the period from June 30, 2000 to July 1, 2019.

Bev McArthur also spoke about the bill in parliament. The politician said she, sadly, knew what it was like to outlive a child. "I know that to lose a child… a son not able to reach his 30th birthday, is the most traumatic event you can ever confront." Her son Andrew was killed when he was hit by a car while cycling. "We must do better for all those people who have lost their loved ones in these extraordinarily tragic circumstances." Politician Fiona Patten said she remembered the day she first got behind the wheel of a car. "I just thought 'this could kill me.' Then what actually struck me as even worse and even more frightening was 'I could kill someone with this. This car is a weapon.'" Ms Patten said she supported the changes in the bill for this reason, as it would expand the legislation to acknowledge that cars are sometimes used as weapons. "In some ways it is surprising that if someone has been charged with murder, attempted murder, gross violence, kidnapping, or carjacking their licence has not been automatically suspended prior to now." She said she was pleased the bill would change that.

Politician Dr Catherine Cumming said she understood why Jeynelle had been upset and frustrated to see the person who had killed her son out driving while on bail. She said she believed community members wanted more justice for victims and more serious penalties for serious offences. "They do not want people to get away with it," Dr Cumming said. "They do not want people to feel that they can have the nerve, on bail, to drive to court. It is very disrespectful. We need to take these measures to make sure they understand that they should not be walking away freely." The bill was passed 37 to 2. Finally a win for Tyler.

Jeynelle and Josh recalled it was a long, tiring day in parliament but they wouldn't have changed a thing. Bittersweet is the best word to describe how they felt. "Obviously you sit back and think, I wish we didn't have to do this at all," Jeynelle said. "For us to push this through, it means we had to lose Tyler. I would do anything to have him back." However, she said she was pleased so many politicians had supported it. "They realised these little loopholes meant that killer drivers could stay on our roads and put so many people's lives at risk. They knew they had to slam the loophole shut and it's a relief they've taken it as seriously as they have." Jeynelle said she would be forever grateful to each and every person who signed the petition. "We wouldn't have been able to do this without them." She said each moment spent on pushing to change the law was to ensure other families didn't have to go through what she and her loved ones did. "All of this was for Tyler. None of it came from me being bitter, vindictive or angry but for my absolute love of Tyler and knowing he deserves better and for other families who will face this. I did it so I know they won't have to pull up at a set of traffic lights and see the person who killed their [loved] one behind the wheel driving." Jeynelle said she hoped her son would have been proud of her efforts. "I think he would be smiling and I think he would be so happy for me," she said. "I can hear his voice saying 'You go get them Mum.'"

Chapter 17

The hundreds of hours Jeynelle and Josh had spent writing to politicians, updating the petition, responding to comments, and updating the Justice for Tyler Facebook page had finally paid off. Jeynelle said while it was a difficult journey, she never considered giving up. "I've been a fighter for my kids their whole lives so I wasn't going to give up now. There were days where I would have a good cry, yell about it all, and then Josh would give me a hug, wipe my eyes, and ask if I was ready to get back to it. The answer was always yes." Jeynelle said she would be forever grateful to the work of politicians including Tania Maxwell, Stuart Grimley, Lisa Neville, Jaala Pulford, and Luke Donnellan in drafting and getting the bill passed. "Tania Maxwell has been the absolute driving force behind these changes and deserves praise."

Ms Maxwell, like Jeynelle, wants to ensure any loopholes are "slammed shut." "To this day she is still messaging me with updates on the Road Safety bill to make sure it has not overlooked cases like Tyler's on technicalities. She is in touch with Lisa Neville's office to make sure there are no exceptions.

Another shining light in the darkest period of Jeynelle and Josh's lives is Darren Williams, a Detective Sergeant from the Major Collision Investigation Unit. He—unlike many others—fought to ensure he did all he could to present the facts to the jury. Facts that many, but sadly not the jury, thought were surely evidence of guilt.

"The stories that were shared that night [in parliament] by people who have lost loved ones, friends, and constituents who felt that the crime was not being treated with the same level of gravitas that it deserves was unexpected and gave us some consolation. When the bill was passed everyone stood and clapped. Josh hugged me while I cried with relief."

For Josh, it was nice to also be acknowledged for his role in changing the law. At times he felt pushed to the side by the media who were desperate to speak to Tyler's grieving mother. But he was grieving too. He loved Tyler with all his heart. Josh said it was disappointing to often be referred to simply as Jeynelle's partner—as if his status as stepfather somehow made his grief less important. He was even mistakenly referred to on occasion as one of Jeynelle's sons.

"I'm very proud of [Jeynelle]," Josh said. "She's fought very hard to get the changes made—we both have. What Jeynelle has done has been incredible. She's changed the law, she's made both the police and judges approach these cases differently and that's extraordinary." Josh said parliament put aside a day to hear the couple's concerns and the bill was passed with a majority vote, proving the changes were common sense. "People are starting to wake up to not only car crime, but how pathetic car crime is being handled, or rather mishandled, in the courts."

Jeynelle said the couple finally felt that Tyler's life meant something to others. Sadly, that's not how they felt in the courtroom. "It was about highlighting a crime that costs lives and could happen to any of us." Jeynelle said she and Josh wanted to highlight the injustice of how victims and their families were treated by the justice system. "To not even have your licence removed after being charged with killing a person and driving off? The one comment we saw over and over again on the petition, Why isn't this already the law?"

Jeynelle isn't stopping now. Another change she is working for is the laws surrounding jury deliberations. "I believe all jury deliberations should be recorded and a copy given to the

Office of Police Prosecutions after the verdict has been announced," she said. "If it is found that the decision is not based on the evidence presented and not based on law then the OPP should get the chance to appeal a not guilty verdict." Jeynelle also believes a copy should be provided to the judge and the defence team. She has spoken to a number of politicians about this.

Jeynelle also thinks mandatory sentences should be imposed for hit and run drivers, but she doubts this will ever happen. "It's hard enough to get a guilty verdict if they plead not guilty," she said. "The chances of them introducing mandatory sentencing is way out of reach and will remain so until society takes car crime seriously instead of a whoops, glad it didn't happen to me."

Chapter 18

Tyler's family and friends ensure his memory is kept alive every way they can. Each year they get together for a cruise for Tyler. They share memories about him and laugh at how he always found himself in some sort of trouble. Oaklee and the Leamer family named a star in Tyler's honour—a gesture that Jeynelle and Josh will be forever grateful for. "Tyler now has his very own star in the sky," Jeynelle said. "Our beautiful superstar."

On the one-year anniversary of Tyler's death, Jeynelle posted a photo of her hugging her precious boy. "My baby Tyler," she wrote. "It's so hard typing this knowing that you won't send me a reply with a cute emoji and you signing off with I love you," she wrote. "Today marks 12 long months since you were stolen from us and it feels cruel that it has gone by so fast. I am never going to stop missing you, loving you, thinking of you and fighting for you. You were the light in my darkest hours, my strength when I was falling and —along with your brother Samuel—my reason for breathing each and every day." She told Tyler he was always loved, never forgotten, and forever missed. "I miss Tyler like crazy," mate Joshua Hames wrote.

Melanie Leamer said Tyler would be proud of his mum. "The way you keep putting one foot in front of the other, you certainly are an inspiration to many. Your whole family is. Sending you the biggest hugs to help you through this day." Jeynelle's friend Bianca Carter said everyone who knew Tyler missed him every day. "Keep watching over us all because we know you are there," Bianca wrote. "You're gone but you will never be forgotten."

In April 2019, Jeynelle and Josh presented the first Tyler Dean scholarships to two Gordon TAFE students. It was a proud moment. The $500 scholarships are awarded to students overcoming hardship who show commitment to their studies.

Jeynelle said she would be forever grateful to Adam Fratantaro from Diversitat for putting Tyler on the path to becoming a panel beater. "Tyler was so disconnected from mainstream school and I asked him to go for one meeting when he turned 18 just to see if he could find something to do rather than sit at home," she said. She said that meeting was a turning point in Tyler's life. "He was in a certification course within a week," she said. When he graduated, Adam ensured he had a suitable outfit and drove him around to businesses to submit resumes. "After Tyler was stolen, Diversitat sent a beautiful bouquet and Adam sent a card with a heartfelt letter about his time with Tyler." He then set up the annual Tyler Dean Student of the Year Awards. "It's an honour and we are forever grateful to Adam and Diversitat for all they did for Tyler," Jeynelle said.

On December 16, 2019, Jeynelle told her Facebook friends that she had made the tough decision not to hold a 21st birthday party for Tyler. "Instead of having a 21st birthday for Tyler, because let's face it, I would just sob and be a mess the whole time, I would rather everyone celebrate in their own way and post a pic of you raising a glass, stubby, shot (whatever) so I can save it and put it in a 21st photo frame. Party your butts off please," she wrote. She said Tyler had been looking forward to celebrating his 21st birthday since he was 10. "I will raise a glass and cheers to your beautiful Tyler," Katie Woodfield wrote. "I will raise a glass to your beautiful son," wrote Natalie Mitchell.

On January 2, 2020, Tyler should have been celebrating his 21st birthday. He no doubt would have been surrounded by mates and enjoyed a bourbon or two. "Happy heavenly 21st birthday," Jeynelle wrote on her Facebook page. "Words cannot express how much I wish you were here. You brought so much joy and grey hairs into my life and I will love and miss you forever." A large group visited Tyler at his garden at the Geelong cemetery.

Melanie Leamer posted her sadness that Tyler wouldn't get to celebrate the milestone. "I should be sitting down wondering how drunk and what trouble you and Oaklee are going to get into after celebrating your 21st birthday," she wrote. "Instead, some of your friends met up at the beach to make a toast for you for a birthday you'll unfortunately never have. Then off to the cemetery to cut the cake they got for you and share it amongst themselves and with your family out there." Melanie said Tyler was loved by many. "You'll never be forgotten," she wrote. "Happy 21st birthday Tyler. We all wish you were here to celebrate with."

Jeynelle's wish of a memento of the day was realised when dozens of photos flooded in and the Leamer family presented her and Josh with a 21st birthday key for Tyler signed by his friends. "Smiles can be hard to find on these days," Jeynelle said. "It should have been a hired hall, loads of love, laughter, and loud music, the embarrassing photo montage and Tyler shaking his head and covering his eyes. Instead—broken hearts."

Oaklee will never be able to forget the night he lost one of his best mates. He will forever be haunted by it. One shining light for him is his young son, who he named Tyler to honour his late friend. Shortly after Tyler's death, Oaklee found out his girlfriend Sophie Higham was pregnant. She said it gave Oaklee something to look forward to at the worst time of his life. "He approached Jeynelle and asked if he could name his child in honour of his best friend Tyler," Sophie said. On July 9, 2018, Tyler Eric Leamer was born.

His parents are amazed at how similar he is to his namesake. "Tyler was always a go getter,

Jeynelle would say, and our Tyler is too,"
Sophie said. "He's always on the run, getting
into things and up to no good at times. When
he falls over he gets up and gives it another
go. He's got no fear." Sophie said Tyler and
Oaklee were "always up to no good. They were
always out riding motorbikes or having a few
drinks." Sophie remembers that she would
sometimes complain that Oaklee spent more
time with Tyler than her. "I'd get annoyed,"
she laughed. "But I would do anything for
that to happen again." Sophie said the two
were inseparable. "Where ever Oaklee went,
he went too." She said when the pair weren't
out riding bikes they enjoyed catching the
train to Geelong and hanging out. Sophie said
Oaklee was devastated by the loss of his best
mate. "He misses him so much," Sophie said.
But their little Tyler is his saving grace.

Despite the law change, Jeynelle, Josh,
and Samuel have been robbed of so many
things. Special occasions will never be the
same. They could always count on Tyler to be
at any event, no matter what else he had going

on. Jeynelle will never again find a stray Post-it note with a simple message from her blue-eyed boy such as 'Love ya mum.' Josh won't be able to watch El Dorado with his stepson and mate by his side, and watching *Alien* will only convey painful memories for Samuel.

Josh misses Tyler's unparalleled energy, the sound of him barging in the back door at all hours of the night, and their blokey banter. "I'd offer him a scenario i.e., just imagine if you were in a bakery and you were caught pressing down on cakes to judge their moistness." Then Josh would keenly await one of Tyler's clever answers. He said his stepson was energetic, boisterous, and obnoxious (but in an endearing way). Josh will miss him insisting that a sav in batter at 3am is a must-have and commenting, "Mad as bro!" or "Boss as."

Josh's mum Di misses playing Cards Against Humanity as a family. She misses the laughter that would fill the air whenever Tyler was around. She tends to his garden at the Geelong cemetery, marvelling at the dozens of cards, trinkets, and flowers that adorn it. There's even a half full bottle of bourbon in a tree near his garden. It's been there for a few years, Di said. A gift from a mate for Tyler. "I go and water the garden and think of Tyler," Di said.

Tyler's grandmother Ellen smiles every time she looks at Tyler's photo that takes pride of place in her lounge room. She talks to her grandson often and was elated to be sent a sign from him that he was watching over her. "He hasn't gone far," she said. "I'd like to see him but I know he's here." Ellen said she started finding tiny white feathers all over the house. Then she found bigger ones. She learnt that angels send white feathers to make people aware of their presence. It's something she can't entirely comprehend, but she knows it's a sign from heaven. "It means a lot. I know he's thinking of [me] and saying, 'Nan, I'm here with you.'"

Sam Bushby also goes to the garden regularly. "I go there a lot, especially when I'm feeling down." He will never forgive Glynn for taking his best mate. And he's livid Glynn and his family have never attempted to apologise. "He should have apologised," Sam said. "His family should have apologised. Defend your son but also apologise for his wrongdoing. It's not fair."

Jeynelle will miss the hilarious tales she was constantly told about her son's antics. She will also miss watching horror movies with him. "He loved Child's Play when he was younger," she said. "His prep teacher called me in one day because he was chasing other kids around the yard making stabbing motions and saying 'Chucky wanna play?' She didn't find it nearly as funny as I did."

Jeynelle talks to her son often. "If I do something silly I tell him not to laugh at me," she said. "I talk to him when a song he likes comes on the radio, when I walk past his room, before I go to sleep, when I look at his pictures. I feel him around me always." And in a sign of love from above, Jeynelle knows that if she is really feeling down, Tyler will ensure the song *Time After Time* is played on the radio.

Chapter 19

The hole in the heart of Tyler's brother Samuel will never be repaired. The now 29-year-old is devastated his brother won't be by his side when he marries his fiancé Juliana Santos-Oliveira. When asked what he misses most about his younger brother, he doesn't hesitate for a second. "Everything," he replies. He admits the two were like chalk and cheese but it didn't matter. They had an unbreakable bond. Samuel often had to cover for his brother if he found himself in trouble. "He most certainly got into mischief and I was usually there to help him out. He would say, 'Don't tell mum, but I did this.'" Samuel said he loved being an older brother and father figure to Tyler. "I used to help take care of him, change his diapers," Samuel said. His mum was on her own until she met Josh and she experienced some tough times. "Mum was going through a very stressful time so I helped however I could." Samuel taught Tyler how to do most things, including how to ride a bike. Samuel, a self-confessed homebody, said Tyler loved getting out and spending time with his mates. "He was an ultra extrovert," Samuel said. "He was hardly ever home. He was either out with mates or they were at our house." The two fought like most brothers do. Samuel said they would both throw punches, but he as the older brother would be the one who got in trouble. They called each other dumbass.

Samuel recalled he had to talk Tyler out of sending in a video to the television show

Jackass. He recalls Tyler had plans to do some sort of a stunt on his skateboard. "He had a knack of getting himself into trouble," Samuel laughed. One time he was caught driving a rider mower through the streets of Winchelsea. "It was never anything serious, but he did get in trouble a lot."

Samuel remembers that, right before he died, Tyler excitedly rang him to tell him he had got a job as an apprentice. "He wouldn't shut up about it," Samuel remembers. "I said 'good on you' and I told him I would see him on Sunday.'" But he would never hear his brother's voice again. On the night Tyler was hit and killed Samuel and his fiancée had gone to bed early. Samuel's phone was on silent and the dozens of calls from his mum went unanswered. "To say I was devastated is an understatement," Samuel said. "It's hard to put into words but the best way I can describe it is you lose all feeling. It's like you're at a point where you could stab yourself in the hand with a knife and you wouldn't feel it. You just feel numb." Samuel drove to Winchelsea the next day and he, Josh, and Jeynelle sat and told stories about Tyler. "There were lots of tears," he remembers.

Samuel said he already had a pessimistic view about the Australian justice system before Tyler's death. But now he views it as a joke. "When I found out I was not surprised," he said. "I was angry of course, but not surprised. The only thing that stopped me from doing something stupid was thinking about my fiancée." Samuel said he watched with disgust as Glynn walked out of the court after the ruling was handed down. "I watched him walk out and he smiled," Samuel said. "He was smiling, he was happy, he got away with it." Samuel said the country's justice system needed to be entirely overhauled. "The whole system needs to be burnt to the ground. There are people getting killed in hit and runs every day and people are getting away with it. A hard restart is what we need." Samuel also said Glynn's $650 fine was a joke. "Right now you can get into more trouble for breaching the coronavirus restrictions than you can for killing someone with your car. As Tyler would say, 'That's fucked up.'" Samuel said family gatherings would never be the same. He said the best way to describe them now was "quiet. When there was an important occasion he was always there," Samuel said. "Now there is an empty seat that shouldn't have been empty for 80 years. I think about him every single day."

Jeynelle has good days and bad days. She smiles countless times a day when something reminds her of Tyler. On particularly trying days she recites three lines of her favourite Robert Frost poem. It just about sums up how she feels. The woods are lovely, dark and deep, But I have promises to keep, And miles to go before I sleep....